D1707769

Bankmules
The Story of Van Lear, a Kentucky Coal Town

"When steam locomotives ruled the day…" This old line drawing was first used in a History of the **Consolidation Coal Company, 1864 - 1934**. It is reproduced here with the permission of ConsolEnergy, the successor company.

Bankmules

The Story of Van Lear, a Kentucky Coal Town

by
James E. Vaughan

Jesse Stuart Foundation
Ashland, Kentucky
2003

ISBN: 1-931672-25-3

Book and Cover Design by
Designs on You!

Published by:

Jesse Stuart Foundation
1645 Winchester Avenue • P.O. Box 669
Ashland, Kentucky 41105
(606) 326-1667
JSFBOOKS.com

Table of
Contents

This hand-drawn map shows some of the roads, railroads, streams, houses, and other sites in Van Lear around 1920 - 1940. Located southeast of Paintsville, the Johnson County seat, the town was laid out along Miller's Creek, from the Levisa Fork of the Big Sandy River at West Van Lear to the Number 5 mine and Butcher Hollow, a distance of about five miles. The Miller's Creek Railroad was financed by a close friend of Franklin Delano Roosevelt, a man named Van Lear Black, whose Fidelity & Trust Company provided funds to build the main line and sidings at each of the five mines. The town was named for Mister Black. The railroad and mine buildings are no longer standing. Except for private homes, the old #5 store, and the company office building, few of the original structures remain. The Van Lear Historical Society has undertaken to save something of the town's history by collecting and preserving artifacts in their Miners' Museum. A model of the town as it existed in the 1930s is now found on the third floor of the office building.

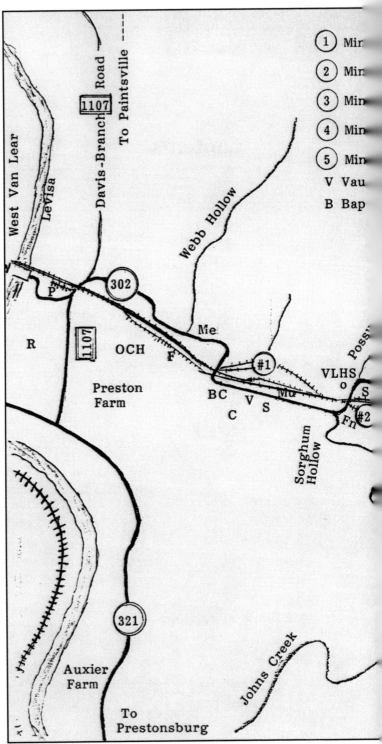

LEGEND   VAN LEAR AS WE KNEW IT

P   power plant   C   cabin site
R   River area   Mu mule barn
OCH old Clubhouse   VLHS Historical Society / Museum
F   football field   St main store
Me Methodist Church   Fn fountain or rec building
BC Bradley Crossing   CH club house   SS Silk STocking Row
S   Sparks   H   high school building

urch Ho hotel   G Central Grade School   Pr Priest's house

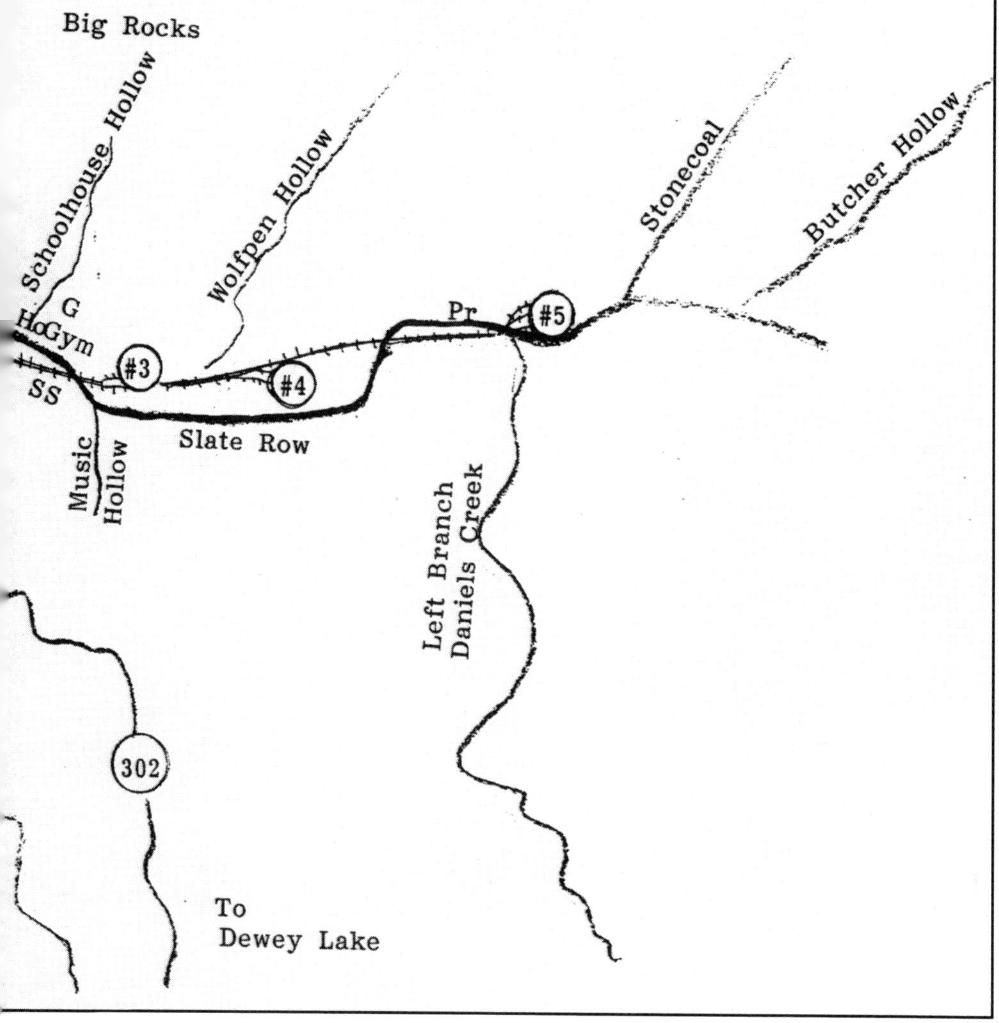

Big Rocks

Schoolhouse Hollow

Wolfpen Hollow

Stonecoal

Butcher Hollow

G
Ho Gym
Pr
#5

#3
#4
SS

Slate Row

Music
Hollow

Left Branch
Daniels Creek

302

To
Dewey Lake

Dedication

To Wanda Lee Rice Vaughan,
my wife of more than half a century,
who inspires me with her gentleness,
and who loves my old hometown and its people as much as I do.

Introduction

BANKMULES is mostly a celebration of a boyhood in a coal-mining town in eastern Kentucky, a nostalgic look back to a time and place that exists only in memory. While a great deal of research preceded my writing, time and distance have clouded my vision, and although I have endeavored to base the story on fact as much as possible, some particulars in my reportage of baseball, basketball, and football games may have been borrowed from one event and merged into another. I have changed names when I was uncertain of the actual identity of individuals. I also invite the reader's indulgence as I attempt to depict what may have transpired on the ill-fated morning of July 17, 1935.

As I read and re-read the literature of this bygone era, the more convinced I became that I should tell this personal story. And I wanted to tell it as truthfully as I could, not only from the perspective of a young boy, but also from that of the miner and mine owner as well as from that of the adult that young boy became. As I reminisced and wrote, I realized that two kinds of conflicts of interest existed back then, perhaps two of the few things that have survived intact over the years. The first was the conflict which existed between the miner and his employer, mostly socio-economic in nature. The second had to do with the perceived differences in "town" folk and "coal camp" folk. We always resented anyone referring to our town as a "coal camp" since we regarded it as superior to shoddier coal-mining villages, and even to county seat towns like Paintsville. Those of us who grew up in Van Lear could be quite snobbish too, as for example, in our preferences for "big band" music, and our denial of the indigenous "country" music of our region. While these conflicts and differences were usually benign, they could also be quite hurtful to the targeted person, somewhat akin to the different chicken in the pen being pecked by the other chickens, who were more alike in color or other perceived quality. In more recent times, children shooting children has focused attention on a similar problem which, apparently, is no closer to a solution than it was in my youth. At least our social differences were handled in a more civil manner.

Much of the literature on life in the coal towns of southern Appalachia tends to focus on poverty and ignorance, almost as though there were no other kinds of mining towns. I hope that I have succeeded to some degree in showing another kind of coal town and way of life. Finally, in the early 1980s, almost thirty years after the founding coal company abandoned the town, former residents rallied behind a small group of people who were determined to preserve something of Van Lear's past. It is perhaps this aspect of the town and its short history that is most noteworthy, most deserving of our attention.

The photographs in this book came from a variety of sources, including Peggy Beers; Jim Cook; Darlene Sparks Preston and her sister Sue Sparks Estep; Warren "Tubby" Harris; the late Silva Lyon; Joyce McCallister Meade; Nicky Pelphrey; Bill Rucker; Janis Goble Taylor; Tom Wills; Stanley Wood; and from the archives of the Consolidation Coal Company and the Van Lear Historical Society, as well as my own personal collection. If you should decide to visit Van Lear, write before hand to arrange for one of the volunteers to show you the old office building, now the Miners' Museum and the repository of many artifacts and memories of a bygone era. Write to Van Lear Historical Society, Post Office Box 369, Van Lear, Kentucky 41265.

James Vaughan

Chapter One
The Baseball Excursion

"The moonlight is the softest, in Kentucky.
summer days come oftest, in Kentucky."
—James Mulligan

It is near daybreak on a very special day, a Sunday morning in July. The year is 1934. The place is West Van Lear at the junction of two railroads. We will soon embark on an excursion, a special trip by railroad coach. Our destination is Cincinnati, the Queen City, our objective a baseball doubleheader between the Cincinnati Reds and the Saint Louis Cardinals. If I'm lucky, my hero, Pepper Martin, will be playing the hot corner. On the tiny station's platform a small group has gathered, mostly men, some dressed in coat and tie, many with summer hats, all rabid baseball fans, and all employed in some capacity by the Consolidation Coal Company, at the mines in Van Lear. My father and I are two of those who wait. For me—and, I suspect, for many of these men—the wait is interminable, the excitement almost unbearable. These men have labored all week, many of them deep within the bowels of the earth. This will be one of the major events of the summer. Baseball is a big thing here.

Nervous and chilly, I jump around in the cool morning air and search the fogbound scene for someone my age, but I seem to be the only kid here. Oh well, I'm thinking, maybe there'll be others like me on the train. It is so cool I pull at my long-sleeved shirt and hug myself for warmth. The cap I am wearing has earpieces, and I pull these down over my ears, although it makes me look sort of goofy.

Later in the day the sun will boil down upon us, and I will roll the sleeves of my white shirt up to the elbows, just like many of the men will do, and I will remove the flop-eared cap and try to look all grown-up. I'm glad that Dad told Mom it was time to get me out of those knickers, and put me in long britches like his. I notice that some of the men are wearing caps like mine, except they don't have those goofy-looking ears, while others, like my dad, are sporting board-stiff straw hats. I recently read that those kinds of hats—they call them "boaters"— are now out of fashion, having been replaced with the lighter Panama. I read that in a magazine while I was waiting to get a haircut at Dave Kelly's Barber Shop. My best friend, Richard Sparks, and I read a lot, and sort of compete to see who can outdo the other. We argue about some of the things we read, but they're always friendly arguments. I must remember to tell him about the hats.

I dance up and down, trying to stay warm in the early morning fog, glancing now and then down the dimly lighted cinder path, still hoping Richard or some of my other buddies will show up with their dads. A car has stopped down below, a bootlegger making a delivery of some moonshine to one of the men in our group. The smell of homemade whiskey now mingles with coal smoke from the kitchen fires in the heavy morning air, and man-talk grows louder with each drink they take. The smell of whiskey reminds me of the time Richard and I got into some of his dad's stuff, and mixed it with some root beer, and we got sort of light-headed and tipsy, and then I remember another time when we were down at Webb Hollow and it was a hot day and the corks kept popping off of some bottles of home brew that one of the men had set out on a backyard fence.

We had been waiting for what seemed to me an eternity when, all of a sudden, the full-throated sound of the passenger train's steam whistle comes out of the foggy distance, and for a moment the whole group just stands there, frozen. Then in an instant, all of us react as one, chattering away, excitedly moving about, glad that the long wait is finally ending. The sound resonates once more, and then a third time, louder each time, adding to our excitement. The melodious trumpet of the steam-powered engines that pull the passenger trains is like no other sound on God's earth. In contrast to the croupy whine of the coal train, the passenger engine's sound is one of a kind and hard to describe, brassy and musical, sometimes even sort of mournful, but especially to a young boy like me, it is magical, upbeat. It holds out the promise of another kind of life, one that hints of great and wondrous things to come, and I know that I will be treated to a brief glimpse of some of those things this very day.

The great whistle blares forth again, cleaving the foggy stillness with its Gabrielesque resonance, like a trumpet heralding the second coming. The sound echoes through the hills and down the valleys. It reverberates through the fog-shrouded morning air once more, louder this time, first at Blockhouse Bottom, and then as it passes the Auxier and Preston farms, homes of descendants of Samuel Auxier, who was one of the very first settlers in our part of Kentucky.

The Van Lear steam-electric plant with the old bridge over the Levisa Fork of the Big Sandy River at the right, and Cap Duncan's barn and home in between the two structures, c. 1914.

John M. "Cap" Duncan, and his grandson, Arlo Wallace, standing in front of the recreation building at Van Lear. It was Cap Duncan who guided J. C. C. Mayo to coal outcroppings up and down the Levisa Fork of the Big Sandy River. After his marriage to my cousin Evelyn Hammond, Arlo worked in the Consol main store, where he kept production records and issued scrip to Van Lear miners.

The train rounds the bend, its headlight flashing, and in its light I get a brief glimpse of the roof of Cap Duncan's big riverside home. Cap Duncan is John M. Duncan, Arlo Wallace's, and Anna Mary and Louise Duncan's Granddad. Dad told me that Cap Duncan once captained a riverboat and helped a man named Mayo find outcroppings of coal all up and down the Big Sandy River. That's our river, the Levisa Fork of the Big Sandy, not as big as the Nile or the Mississippi, but just as important, at least in my mind. If I brag a bit I hope you will forgive me. I love this part of the world, and I want everyone to know about it.

Steam gushes in great white torrents as the brightly polished engine passes us by and moves on. It stops and we prepare to board one of the eight olive green coaches. The normal complement of coaches on the twice-daily runs up and down the Big Sandy Valley is three—four at most! Boy, oh boy! Eight! This has to be special! As we get ready to board the train, I ask my dad if the locomotive is a Pacific or a Berkshire, but he ignores me and hoists me up to the vestibule.

We enter the coach and find a seat, and I search the crowd, hoping to spot a young boy like myself among the throng, someone to while away the time with on the train. Maybe we could play paper-rock-scissors or some other game. And we could talk and compare ideas about baseball. But, no such luck. There are just the men and a couple of women, so I stare out the window, trying hard to see the little house we had lived in for a short time a few years ago. The pale yellow glow of a street lamp lights up the front of a store, barely visible through the fog, and I am reminded of the day my brother George let me go with him to that store, and how they had watermelons and cantaloupes, and I told the man that I would sing "The Big Rock Candy Mountain" for him if he would give me a watermelon, but he said, no, he couldn't do that, but he would give me a cantaloupe if I would sing it. I shook my head and pointed at the fruit, indicating that I would sing only for a watermelon. On the way home, I changed my mind and told George that I would go back and sing for the cantaloupe, but he wouldn't take me back. I wasn't quite three then. I am now almost nine, and not so bold. I probably wouldn't sing for either of them today.

That's me and my wagon at West Van Lear Junction, wearing the coat I wore to the Al Smith train, but without the Herbert Hoover button, a month or so after the 1928 presidential election, following a snowfall.

Later that same year, two men named Herbert Hoover and Al Smith were campaigning for the presidency, and our whole family went to meet a special train that stopped at our little train station, while some politicians gave speeches. The reason I remember this so well is because I insisted on wearing a Hoover button on my coat. It sort of embarrassed everyone since the people on that train were campaigning for their Al Smith, a Democrat. My man, the Republican Herbert Hoover, won the presidency in 1928, and I was sure that I had helped elect him by wearing his button.

"All aboard!" the conductor calls out, interrupting my daydream. He reaches for the portable step, and waves to the engineer and, with a rush of air, a chug or two and a puff of steam, we are on our way. I sit there, bug-eyed with excitement. Nothing can be better than this trip to see the Reds and Cards play! Nothing! Not even Coney Island or Camden Park. I just wish some of my buddies were here to share it with me.

I turn my attention back to our coach. The men are now laughing and shouting to one another and to old friends and relations who have boarded earlier at Elkhorn City and Pikeville, or from towns on left or right Beaver Creek. All are involved in some way with the coal-mining industry. Busy milling about, the men leave the two women to themselves. One of the women is a real snappy looker and, I'm guessing that she is the girl friend of a young, single man, both out for a fling. Maybe both women are wives, and if they are, they will now surely acquire a bad reputation back home. It's a man's world here in eastern Kentucky. My mom would never go on a train trip like this one. She said so before we left home this morning, but she also said she was glad I could go. She understands this is a man thing, and, as we were leaving, she told me and Dad to watch out for bad strangers, whatever that means.

I know how lucky I am that Dad saw fit to bring me along with him on this excursion. Money is tight here in the eastern Kentucky coal country. There had been talk about how we might escape what they are calling the Great Depression, but now they say there is too much coal on the market, and too little demand for it. Because Van

My mother, Frances Lynk Vaughan, shortly before her marriage to my father, Jim Vaughan.

Lear's Miller's Creek coal is one of the world's best domestic heating coals, her Consol mines remain open more than some of the others, but now that it's summer, there's less demand for heating coal, and that's why Dad and his fellow miners worked only three days last week.

I should tell you something about myself, I guess. I was named for my father, and he in turn was named for his father's father, who was James, son of Thomas, who was the eldest son of William and Fereby Vaughan. That's as far back as we can go with our family tree on my dad's side of our family, although last summer when Granddad Anthony Wayne Vaughan visited with us, I recall that and he and Dad and Cousin Willie, who came to see us from Tampa, Florida, talked about how old William had been a Welshman who traded with Cherokee Indians, and they talked about how our people came from a clan of Vaughans who lived for centuries at a place called Tretower in southern Wales, but no one seemed to know exactly who the first male Vaughan was in this country. I thought of all this when Dad returned to our seat, and I wondered if he would tell me more about his side of our family, for I knew that next school term Miss Hobson would have us write our family histories as a school project. Dad had never been as keen on family matters as his father, so maybe I should talk some more about it to Granddad. Still, I'm thinking, maybe Dad can tell me some more things I want to know. I hesitate a minute and then, with him sitting right there next to me, I swallow hard, and ask him point-blank. "What was your grandma like, Dad?" There! I had asked it. And now he's sitting there, looking at me for what seems like the longest time, probably wondering why I hadn't asked him something about baseball.

"Grandma Vaughan?" he asks me at last, still looking at me sort of funny. When I nod, he hesitates, and then he says, "I didn't know her well, son. I only saw her the few times when she and Grandpap visited us at Winslow." That's all he says at first, but when I keep looking up at him, he decides to tell me more.

"Her name was Susannah Wilson," he says. "I don't remember too much more about her, but I can tell you a bit about Grandpap. He was sickly as a boy. He and Pap— my dad, your granddad, that is—kept horses for the Union army at South Point, Ohio, during the Civil War. Pap used to talk a lot about that. It was 1863 and he was only fifteen years old. The two of them took the government ferry from Catlettsburg across the Ohio River to the point every work-day."

That was more than I expected him to tell me. I don't ask any more about his grandmother, especially about her being part Cherokee Indian, which is what Granddad told me, but Dad never wanted to acknowledge that we had any Indian blood in our family, even though it was pretty well known that old William's wife, Fereby, was part Cherokee too. But, like I've been telling you, Dad didn't much care to talk about it. Indian features showed up most in me and Uncle Everett. Granddad told me that many a man took as his mate a young Indian maiden. John Looney was one. My great-great-great-grandfather, William Vaughan, a Welshman, married John's granddaughter, Fereby Benton, and that's how we got some of our Cherokee Indian blood. Granddad had told me that last year, and he said his mother, Susannah Wilson, also had Cherokee blood. Although Granddad had told me all of this earlier, I decide that I would say no more about it to Dad. Instead, I switch to a question about his mother, whose maiden name was America McBrayer.

"What was your mother like, Dad?" I ask, hoping he won't mind telling me more about her, since I already know that she was mostly Scottish, and probably had no Indian blood in her line.

"Ma Vaughan?" he asks, smiling as he says it. "She was a fine lady. Her family lived in Carter County, and Ma's dad was named William McBrayer. I didn't get to know any of the other McBrayers."

Even this much information was special. What my father was telling me was really rare for him, and I sat there all bug-eyed, listening intently, wondering if that was a trace of whiskey I smelled on his breath. Maybe that was why he was telling me so much. Maybe booze had loosened his tongue. Dad was known to take a nip now and then, but not all that often. When he asked me why I was asking all this, I told him about the theme I would have to write next school year.

"You ought to ask Pap to tell you more," Dad says. "He knows a lot of other things about his side of our family," After I told him my reason for my questions, he kept on talking, but without really telling me much more. "Pap'll come to visit us again sometime this summer," he says, and then someone yells out to him, and he turns to see who it is, and that ends our little talk about family.

"Hey, Jim Vaughan," the man says as he comes bounding toward us from the far end of our coach, maneuvering around the other men still standing in the aisle.

"Dave Tufts, you old son of a gun," Dad says, rising from his seat to shake hands. "The last time I saw you, you were just a sprite of a boy, going to school to Maude Childress at Rush."

Dad and the man named Dave Tufts stand there and hang onto each other's hands for what seems like a minute or more as they trade gossip and news about each other and their families. Maude Childress was my Aunt Maude, who married Dad's brother Everett.

The Vaughans and the Tufts and the Childresses grew up together in Boyd County near Ashland. After a bit, Dad turns to me and says, "Dave, this is my youngest. We named him James too, after me and my granddad."

"Hi-dee, Mister Tufts," I say, rising up from my seat and extending my right hand to the man. After Dave Tufts says hello to me, he and Dad exchange a few more pleasantries, and then he moves on down the coach in search of his brother Bill, whereupon Dad sits back down and starts lecturing me.

"Son," he says, "don't say 'hi-dee;' say 'hello' or 'how do you do' but never say 'hi-dee.' It's a childish and unmannerly thing to do." I nod and that was the end of that, but you can be sure that I'll remember it. Dad was always telling me things I should or shouldn't do. My half-sister, Ida Mae, really resented it when Dad told her things like that, but she's now a young woman, twenty years old, and getting ready to move to Covington, along with Miss Hobson's sister Sally, both of them planning to study at Saint Elizabeth's to be registered nurses. I guess she'll be happy to finally escape Dad's constantly correcting her behavior. I don't like it all that much either, but I never say anything about it. Funny, how one thought leads to another. I just recalled one time when I had done something I shouldn't have done, and Dad got out his old razor strop. When I saw the big leather thing in his hand I ran outside, circled the house, and then came back inside and hid under a library table that we had in our living room, and this made Dad even more angry, and he really let me have it with the strop. I bumped my head on a sharp corner of the table, and began to cry and carry on something awful, and this caused Ida Mae to do an unusual thing..

"Stop it, Dad!" she yelled real loud. "You're going to kill him!" Dad had told her to be quiet or she would get it too. It was one of the few times that I recall that she took up for me, and I really appreciated it.

I settle down in my green mohair-like seat as my dad goes off in search of his brother John, and John's sons from Garrett, and other kin and pals from up Beaver Creek. I watch him disappear among the men now standing in the vestibule, and hope I can get his attention again later, as there's lots more that I'd like to ask him about family, and stuff about Van Lear and Ashland.

My father, Jim Vaughan, and his first wife, Ella Hammond Vaughan, holding daughter Ida Mae in her arms. In the foreground are son George and niece Beulah Hammond. This photo was taken around 1916, shortly before the first Mrs. Vaughan's untimely death.

As I sit there alone in my seat, I recall one of the first times I rode a train. It was when Dad brought us to Van Lear. He and my older brother and sister, George and Ida Mae, had lived there once before in 1920, right after Dad's first wife, Ella, died. That makes me and George and Ida Mae only half brother and sister, but we all feel like family. Anyway, they moved back to Ashland, where I was born after Dad married my mom, Frances Burgraf Lynk.

It is not yet daylight, and I sit for a long time, drinking in the luxury of the coach. I examine the mahogany and the brass spittoons in the vestibules, and I remember that the trainmen call passenger trains "varnish." Northbound, the train rolls on. In contrast to the regular runs, the excursion special does not stop at all the local stations, just those that have passengers to pick up. It is still too dark to see outside, but I can tell that we have passed on through the Dawkins station without stopping. "Paintsville," the conductor announces. "Paintsville," he repeats as he walks through the coach, a swagger in his step. "Next stop, Paintsville."

Paintsville, the county seat of Johnson County, had been the final home of that man named Mayo, a man who had made lots of money selling coal rights after Cap Duncan helped him find the outcroppings of the coal seams along the river banks. I remember my father's pointing out the Mayo mansion, and his telling me that the man who built it once taught in a one-room public school at Van Lear, right where the water plant and rec building are now located, back before Van Lear was Van Lear, but he didn't live to see the completion of our town. That man's grandfather, Dad told me, had settled his family on a farm somewhere near West Van Lear.

All sorts of thoughts now race through my mind. I mentally conjure a vision of myself competing for the Van Lear Bankmules against Paintsville's Tigers. The two largest towns in the county maintain separate schools, and their teams are fierce rivals in baseball, football, and basketball. In case you're wondering where our school's nickname came from, my brother George told me that either School Superintendent C.V. Snapp or his predecessor Forest Bell suggested it. The mines were once called "coal banks," and the coal was brought to the surface with small mules. And so the name, "Bankmules."

A rushing sound breaks my reverie.

Steam hisses from the locomotive up ahead as it pauses to take on water before entering the passenger yard. Lights flicker and I can see several men ready to board. In the distance a long, shiny automobile stops, and from it step two elegantly dressed men. They enter the club car attached to the rear of our train, and I can hear some of the men speak of Consol and Northeast and C&O officials. Brass! Big shots! The words are uttered in a sharp, almost mean tone. There are big social differences between men who work with their hands, and men who manage money and companies and other men. No one had to explain that one to me. I just know it. But, despite this, I long to see inside that club car, so with no one noticing me, I get up and sneak to the rear of our car, and go through the door and, on tiptoe, peer inside. It sure is different, with thick carpeting, silvery flasks and bottles, and big, stuffed leather chairs, and a lot of other fancy stuff. But I don't get much of a look, as the conductor has spied me and sends me back to my seat just as the train starts moving once more.

"Jim!" someone calls and I turn, but the man is addressing my father, who is standing at the other end of our car. As the train picks up speed, I return to watching the grown-ups as they meet and greet one another, laughing and lurching down the aisle of the coach, voices raised above the din of the train's clacking wheels. Each time the vestibule door opens, the train sounds grow louder, and the smell of coal smoke enters the car. My father now stands near the lavatory, illuminated by the pale yellow overhead light. He leans against the wall as he talks to Uncle John. The cigar smoke is thick. I tug at the window, hoping to lift it and get a breath of fresh air. My father has seen me do it.

"Don't do that, son," he cautions me. "You'll let cinders in." But it's too late. I have already raised the window, and I now feel the sting of a hot cinder against my cheek. I quickly lower the window, the eyes of my father still upon me, causing me more pain than the cinder.

What's a kid to do, all alone with no one his age to talk to? My thoughts turn back to the hills—mountains, outsiders call them— which we are now leaving behind us. The farther north we go, the smaller the hills. From Johnson County southward the hills grow even more magnificent, but we regard our hills as the best, especially the Big Rocks, two giant monoliths that stand somehow detached from the surrounding ridges, high above Van Lear at the head of Possum and Schoolhouse Hollers, overlooking miles of Appalachian ridges and valleys. The Big Rocks are one of our favorite spots. Last summer Billy's cousin visited him from somewhere up in West Virginia, and we let him go with us to see the rocks. Billy's cousin laughed at our hills. He said that the bluffs above the New River Gorge in his state were higher, but we didn't believe him. Later, Richard said he may have been right, that he had never visited there, but he once saw the Breaks of Sandy near Elkhorn City, and they were higher than our hills.

Actually we have learned a lot about our part of Kentucky from our teachers. Miss Harris once told us that our hills are part of a chain of mountains that stretches all the way from northern Alabama to Canada. Last year I learned that many thousands of years ago the earth buckled, folded, then cracked and split apart all along the Appalachian range. As the folding took place, some parts fell, while others were lifted up, often forming long, parallel ridges. This movement altered the course of rivers. Some of the cracks and fissures we see as we play along the tops of those ridges are the result of those movements of long ago, while others were created more recently when the miners below–our fathers and brothers–removed the final pillars of coal, allowing the mountain to drop.

We don't always admit that we know a lot of stuff, since it isn't wise to act like you know too much, at least around some people. I mean, there's a kind of "good old boy" thing in our part of the world where some people think more of you if you act like you don't know too much. Some outsiders think we are ignorant hillbillies. Well, we're not! And one reason is that we have very good school teachers. The mine managers saw to that by hiring the best teachers they could find, and they did this because their kids go to our schools. Now, you may think I'm bragging, but I'm not. We kids who live and go to school in Van Lear are not ignorant. We read a lot and have learned from our parents and teachers, no matter what that cousin of Billy's may have thought.

The excursion train jerks to a halt. A jolt back to reality! We have stopped at Whitehouse, another small coal camp on the banks of the Levisa Fork. I look out at the rough clapboard houses, and contrast the scene with my own coal town. We move on, and our next stop is at Torchlight. The mines in these towns and at Peach Orchard and Richardson were among the first to be opened and now are mostly worked out, and in the towns the buildings ramshackled, unpainted, rotting, and falling into disrepair. Consol paints our houses and keeps the whole town nice and neat. As I look out at the rundown houses in Torchlight, I can't help but wonder if that same fate awaits my beloved Van Lear. I wonder if this is what happens to all company-owned coal towns.

As we pull into Louisa the eastern sky across the river in West Virginia is becoming lighter. Once more, I listen to the conversation of the men. A man identified as Fred Vinson, who had played on some of Louisa's better town baseball teams, has boarded the train. Old teammates and those who have played against him greet the popular lawyer, now serving his sixth term in our nation's capital as congressman from our district. Years later he will be appointed chief justice of the Supreme Court by President Harry Truman. Today, he is just another baseball fan boarding our train at Louisa. Fred Vinson is a handsome man. He has the long nose and high cheekbones often found on those who have Indian blood. I wonder if he too has Indian blood. And this sets my mind to wondering about Indians and pioneer families and a hundred other things.

Oftentimes, when my buddies and I play along the steep hillsides and ridges, high above the clouds, we think about serious things, like the origins of man, the redman in particular. Just this past fall, my buddy Richard and I were traipsing through the woods, high above town, playing like a couple of wild Indians. Somehow, even as youngsters, we don't quite believe everything we're told in our history books. We suspect that the redman has been wronged. In fact, Richard and I argued that very point one day when we were standing around down at Garland Webb's farm watching them make sorghum molasses. We had both read in our history books that early Spanish and English explorers found the Indians in a wild and un-civilized state, but we questioned this. Richard and I agreed that they—the redmen—discovered us trespassing upon their native land. We even suspect that their civilization was in many ways su-perior to ours, possibly more humane and probably less greedy. At least that's what we thought, but the older people who write our history books seemed to think otherwise.

These thoughts remind me of school, and when I close my eyes I can see our school building, hard against the hills that surround Schoolhouse Holler, and then just as suddenly I can visualize Miss Hobson standing there before me, saying, "James, have you started collecting information for your family theme?"

When I do write that theme, I will need facts about both sides of

The Van Lear Baptist Church and the grade school building are separated by Schoolhouse Holler. At the right is the Midtown Hotel. Music Holler and Slate Row are not visible at the right. This particular photo must have been made around 1920 as the Central Grade School building (center) lacked a section added a year or two later to house a temporary high school.

my family, my father's Vaughans and my mother's Lynks. My thoughts turn to my mother's people and to Kilgore, a town near the Boyd and Carter County line, not far distant from Louisa. Kilgore is the little hamlet where John and Lyda Burgraf Lynk settled when they came down from Butler County, Pennsylvania. I know that we will visit Grandma Lynk there later this year, as we always do, and thoughts of all the fun I'll have now help me while away the time. I remind myself that I must ask Grandma Lynk about where the Lynks and Burgrafs came from when they settled in Pennsylvania, before they came into Kentucky.

The train once more jolts me back to reality. I glance back over my shoulder as we move on. In the distance I can now see the faint outlines of the lock and dam, a device which Dad once told me never did the job it was designed to do, which was to make the Levisa navigable all the way to Paintsville, with another dam to contain the water to a useful depth to Pikeville, a project planned but aborted short of construction, another political boondoggle, Dad called it. We rumble on and more station stops are called out by the conductor "Catalpa...Buchanan...Catlettsburg." The trainman, snappily dressed in his white shirt, black bow-tie, coat and cap, bounds through the coach once more. "Ashland," he intones. "Next stop, Ashland. We'll be in the station for ten minutes at Ashland."

My spirits rise as always with the mere mention of Ashland. I was born at Pollard, not that I remember that event, nor even the two years that followed on 33rd Street. Life always seemed good whenever I thought about Ashland. With a population of some twenty thousand, never to grow much larger, Ashland is arguably past its prime in 1934. At least that was Dad's view of it. Yet, to a youngster like me, accustomed to the comparative isolation of the small communities up Big Sandy, Ashland has all of the allure of a big city. Here and everywhere in 1934, almost everyone holds to the view that small towns and rural areas are inferior. I am thankful that my Dad and I don't believe this. I love Ashland, but I love Van Lear even more. While we Van Learites may have been exempt from put-downs by town folk, those who lived up the creeks and hollers adjacent to our Miller's Creek hamlet were not. Years later, in her personal memoir, *Creeker*, Linda Scott DeRosier would tell how a Paintsville High School cheer derided her and her Meade Memorial athletes and friends with this aspersion: "Two bits, four bits, six bits, a dollar; send those creekers back up the holler!" The word "creeker" was one I never heard while living in Van Lear on Miller's Creek, which lies just over the ridges from Linda Scott's Two-Mile Creek, Greasy Creek, and Boons Camp.

When Dad returned to our seat, I began to quiz him about Ashland and, to my great surprise, he began to tell me some things that he knew about the town. He said that he didn't recall anything about Ashland when it was known as Poage's Settlement. "I'm not that old, son," he said, chuckling with good humor. "I know that Ashland had its beginning in 1854 when the Kentucky Iron, Coal & Manufacturing Company bought property and laid out the town along the Ohio River. I don't have any firsthand knowledge of that, mind you, but I did read about it somewhere. I was born in 1881. Pap—your Granddad—would have been only six years old in 1854, but, knowing him and his memory for things like that, he just might recall something about Ashland's founding. You ought to ask him about it next time he comes visiting."

I glance out the window of our coach, and I can see Clyffeside Park at my left, and I remember being taken there to hear a band concert and something called a Chautauqua when we lived on 33rd Street. I start to ask Dad about that place, but pretty soon the Solvay plant appears at my right, and this reminds me of a story my brother George once told me. Dad's opening up and talking to me again was really something, better than anything like it that I could ever remember between us. Not wanting him to stop, I urge him on. "Tell me some more," I plead with him, hoping he might confirm what George had told me.

"Well," he says, apparently still willing to indulge my curiosity, "there was a man named George Verity who built the world's first continuous steel rolling mill here in 1920, just fourteen years ago. There were other steel mills before his American Rolling Mill, but it was ARMCO that became the biggest employer in Ashland. I never worked for them, but I did work for the Semet Solvay coke plant for a time; they made coke for ARMCO and other steel mills here and up in West Virginia."

After telling me that he had worked at the Solvay plant, Dad was silent for a long moment, and I thought I knew why. My brother George had told me how he had been sent to Dad's supervisor with a note that Dad had written in which he explained that he was ill and wouldn't be able to work one day. The man fired Dad and reported to his superiors that he had received no such note, whereupon Dad had George take him to Solvay and point to the man to whom he had given the note. When he was led to the supervisor, my brother told me that our father, without uttering one word, hit the man with his fist, laying him flat of his back on the coke-blackened Solvay property. The two of them then turned and walked back to our home on 33rd Street. It was shortly after that day in 1927 that my family packed up and moved to West Van Lear. You can bet your sweet life I didn't tell Dad that I knew anything about that incident, but Dad did tell me some more about ARMCO.

Hundreds of young men left their hill farm homes, he said, to work for ARMCO. He described those farms like the one he grew up on at Rush as "rock-pocked subsistence farms," barely able to produce food for the families who lived on them. And he told me that ARMCO offered more in the way of money, but some said ARMCO's domination of the labor market had stifled the city's growth and development. I knew that one of the men who held those views about ARMCO was my dad. Even at age eight, I am inclined to question this, but I didn't say anything about it. I liked Ashland, and the wholesale indictment of capital and management seemed to me to be unfair. Labor had its side—and I knew that my Dad was on the side of labor—but it just seemed to me that more good could be accomplished if labor and management cooperated

An aerial view of Ashland showing the new 13th Street bridge over the Ohio River and the new C&O Railroad passenger terminal in the distance.

with one another. But, what does a kid know? Still and all, I am now vaguely aware that life itself is linear. We can't foresee what lies ahead, neither can we go back and redo what we did in the past. And, of course, no one could possibly have foreseen the consequence had Ashland not attracted George Verity and his ARMCO. I liked what I saw, and it might not have been there without the presence and influence of men like Verity. Of course, I didn't say anything to my father about any of these ideas that morning on the excursion train. Kids just didn't do that sort of thing back then.

Before he got up to take another turn around the coach, Dad told me that he worked a short time for the C&O Railroad, but he said he always felt better deep within a mine where the temperature was cool. He told me about the time he and his father had operated a small coal mine together at Winslow, near Summit in Boyd County, but he said that the benefits offered by a larger coal company and a more modern community were much better and, after a short time with Solvay in 1927, he moved us back to West Van Lear the next year. That's what he told me. He didn't mention the Solvay incident, and I didn't ask about that, but I understood why he preferred Van Lear, which is still neat, even though the men who were mostly responsible for its neatness are no longer there.

I glance out the window and notice that the passenger track has veered away from the freight line, and we are slowly making our way straight through town, down the alleyway between Carter and Central, and I can see people out behind their houses attending to early Sunday morning chores. There were many reasons why I liked Ashland, and I was now looking at some of them. I gaze out at the wide, tree-lined streets, and the space reserved for parks. I always loved Central Park, across from Aunt Min's and Uncle Crockett's, and our train is now passing right behind their house. I strain to see someone I know, but without success, and then I see one of the electric trolleys. I liked to ride in the street cars, and the private cars that they called jitneys. You could hire jitneys to take you anywhere you wanted to go.

I look for the old Union Depot, and then I remember that it was just recently replaced with a handsome new red-brick passenger station, and our train is now coming to a stop under one of its sheltering canopies. When I look away from the window, I am somewhat surprised to find Dad once again sitting there beside me, rather than joining the other men as they make their way to the depot. I decide that I should see if he will tell me more about Ashland. I recall that, before the arrival of ARMCO, Mister Mayo had called Ashland the city where coal meets iron, which seemed to me to be a really neat description.

"What about Mister Mayo, Dad?" I venture, not too sure how to ask it.

"What about him?"

The old Union Depot at 12th Street in Ashland.

"I mean, what do you know about him?"

"Very little, son," he says. "John Caldwell Calhoun Mayo was his name. He used to teach in a one-room school on Miller's Creek. They say that school was located where the old Mine No. 152 coal tipple was built. The water plant and recreation hall are there now, at the mouth of Sorghum Holler. Mayo was the man who bought up and later sold all the coal rights along Miller's Creek. He died in 1914, shortly after building that big mansion in Paintsville. They named US 23 the Mayo Trail in his memory."

With that bit of news, Dad gets up, and looks at me sort of funny-like, and I think I know why. He really doesn't care for all this question and answer business, and I watch as he goes off to the station house in search of Uncle John. I always dreaded the trip on old Route 23, especially the gravel part above Louisa, either on Oak Sparks' Bus Line, or in Chet Staten's car, and I wondered why they didn't name a stretch of this neat railroad for Mister Mayo instead.

I sit at the window and stare out into the early dawn, aware that those two women and I are now the only ones in our coach. I look out once more at the modern city, and contrast it with my coal town. There are big differences, and I wonder who those people were who planned all this, who laid the tracks for the street cars, who planned the wide main thoroughfares, and then paved them with brick, and who decided to light them with gas lamps at night. Who did that? Who were those people?

Three of Dad's brothers, John, Will, and Howard. Of the three, only Uncle John was on the baseball excursion train in July of 1934. At that time, Howard lived in Ashland, where he owned a small grocery store at Pollard. Will had died several years earlier.

The male passengers have started to return from the terminal building. My father and Uncle John and a wad of other miners are now entering our car. When Dad reaches our seat, he is holding a small package, which he places in the luggage rack overhead. He nods and sort of grins at me and takes his seat. The mellow whistle sounds once, twice, a third time, as the train jerks and begins to roll again. The men reclaim their seats. Soon we are passing through the big switching yards at Russell, now filled with C&O, N&W, and L&N hopper cars and gondolas, each loaded with black coal from up Big Sandy. When Dad sees this, he tells me that the market is now glutted, with no ready buyers in sight, and that's why work in the mines was slack. I have heard the men say that what they needed was another industry-wide strike like the one in 1919 which, they said, brought higher wages, but then I also heard them talk about how fuel oil replaced coal during the strike, and now they were worried the same thing would happen again, and I'm thinking it's good to be a boy and not a man and have all those things to worry about.

I start thinking about all that coal, and how it got there, and I recall some of what I learned just last year. Believe it or not, our third grade teacher, Miss Bessie Harris, taught us some things about geology during our last school term. Because of this I have some faint recollection of words such as Precambrian, Paleozoic, Pleistocene, all of which have to do with periods of time back in antiquity. I have a hard time pronouncing the words, but I now recognize them when I hear them or see them in print. My classmates and I know that coal is the region's principal resource, the reason for the coal towns, the source of employment for our fathers and brothers. We know—or at least we were once told—that most of the coal in North America and Europe was formed through successive stages of plant growth, sedimentation, heating, and compression. All of this took place during what geologists call the Carboniferous Period. We know that coal usually begins as peat, becomes something called lignite, and then later changes into either bituminous or anthracite coal. Most of the coal in our region is bituminous or soft coal.

We pick up speed and race on. The tracks now parallel the Ohio River, which seems huge compared to the Big Sandy. We pass through Greenup. I can't see it, but I know that somewhere to my left is a place called "W Hollow," the home of Jesse Stuart. Soon we reach South Portsmouth, then Maysville. The candy butch comes by and I grudgingly spend one of my precious dimes for a Hershey bar. They only cost a nickel at the store in Van Lear. Some of the men are now drinking. Most of them are having a good time. There are no ugly incidents, at least not yet. I glance at my Dad, and start to say something to him. All of a sudden, Dad stands up, and reaches for the package in the overhead rack. He hands the package to me and says, "Here, son. Maybe this will help answer some of your questions about Ashland."

I stare at him, and then eagerly open the package. It's a small book about Ashland, and it has lots of pictures of early scenes and people in it. This will occupy me for the rest of the journey. I guess that's what Dad had in mind when he bought it. When I look up, he is smiling broadly, and then he goes off once more in search of Uncle John.

I look up from the book for the first time since the train departed Maysville, and I discover that we have arrived in Cincinnati! Quickly, I stow the book, put on my cap, making sure the ears are tucked inside, and prepare to get off the train. With a rush of excitement, we enter the great train terminal, merging with a huge throng of people from other excursion trains like ours. They've come from all over Kentucky, Indiana, and Ohio to see the Reds and Cards play. The clock on the wall of the terminal reads straight-up noon as we walk down the main concourse, gawking at the giant mural on the walls of the cathedral-like building. It renders me speechless as I savor its vastness, storing impressions with which to brag and devastate my friends upon our return to Van Lear. My gut has begun to roll. We stop briefly to read the luncheon menu in one of the terminal's cafes. "Forty cents for bean soup!" I hear someone exclaim, his voice echoing throughout the hollow building like he had a giant megaphone or something. "Do you believe that?"

"We don't get that for loading a ton of coal!" my dad says, and I can tell that he means it.

"Forty cents will buy enough beans to feed all of us for a week," another miner adds, and we move on.

Outside the sun is now high in a cloudless sky, the temperature climbing. There are no buses in sight, and taxis charge a dollar a load, so we set out on foot with what is now a small army of people, walking toward Crosley Field. "It's not all that far," someone tells us.

As we walk toward the Reds' hallowed ball park, the mass of people overflows into the street, and I suddenly realize that our journey is taking us right through the center of what many in our group now refer to as "Nigger Town," except I didn't dare say that, not there on the northern side of the Ohio River, even if I felt like using that word, which I didn't, and wouldn't. I might say 'Nigra,' which is the white man's way of saying the more correct word, "Negro," but even that word is now frowned upon by some, and the current and more polite term is "colored" or "person of color." As I look around us, I can see that both blacks and whites live in the neighborhood, but it is mostly black, and this is their territory, not ours. I can hear racial taunts and slurs as we walk along, not from our crowd but from them, the blacks. Dad whispers to me, cautioning me not to stop, not even to look, but to walk straight ahead. And I do just that. A variety of sounds accompanies us as we make our way along the street between the houses. There is the blare of a big band over my right shoulder, a vocal somewhere, a low rumble once in a while and, occasionally, a clear, resonant remark—a racial taunt or slur, usually—and then more music, some tunes that I know, like "Sweet Georgia Brown," "The Dark Town Strutters' Ball," or bluesy things I had never heard before. Real gut-bucket blues, I hear someone call it.

All of a sudden, it occurs to me that I have never heard remarks like the ones just uttered. For the first time in my life I am aware that there is something called racial differences, and I don't like what I am seeing or hearing. And now my thoughts are of the few black people who live in Van Lear, and how seldom we ever see them. In fact, I know of only one black man, a big, strapping man named John, who Mack McKinney said might become a good boxer some day. In fact, Richard and I had heard that Mack had made a date with John to spar with a boxer named Huffy, and we had promised each other that we would go see the two men work out. As we hurry along, I hear another loud voice, and I glance at the others and see that they are intent on walking on through this neighborhood as quickly as possible, and I decide that I will ask Dad about these other things later, not now.

As we continue down the street, I realize that our black people don't act like these people, yet they stay to themselves, perhaps even more severely restricted than these people who live in Cincinnati. Another thought occurs to me. *These* people live in brick houses. They are row houses, side-by-side and fronting onto the street with no green space, but they are brick nonetheless, and we don't live in brick homes. *Their* homes may be better than *ours*, I'm thinking, and just then another taunt is thrown our way by someone with a deep, bass voice, and it sounded like he was saying something about "white trash." I look up and see that Dad and several more men in our crowd are glaring angrily toward the onlookers, who are seated on their porches, watching us and our parade pass by.

I can tell you that I was really glad when we got back into a *regular* neighborhood. In fact, I breathed a big sigh, and I thought I noticed my dad smiling down at me as he loosened his firm grip on my hand. When we reached the ball park, we queued up at a ticket window, where I half expected Mr. Crosley himself to come out to greet us, but, of course, no one did. Instead, we stood in line, jostling and joking, nervously anticipating the day's big games. This Sunday's doubleheader, like most such events, was a sellout and our ticket on the excursion train didn't include admission to the ball park. We settled for seats in the bleachers, far out in right field. As Dad and I passed through the turnstile, the ticket taker handed us a printed program, and I hastily scanned it to see who was scheduled to pitch today's games.

The first game was about to begin as we took our seats in the bleachers, and I strained to recognize faces of players whose pictures I had seen in the newspapers. Chick Hafey had taken up his defensive position in right field immediately in front of us. Some of the fans yelled out his name, and he turned to acknowledge their greeting. Big Ernie Lombardi was behind the plate, Jim Bottomley on first, Tony Piet at second, Gordon Slade at short, and Mark Koenig at third. I wasn't too sure about the other Reds' outfielders, but I heard someone say their names were Comorosky and Pool, or something like that. I studied the Reds' newsletter that the ticket-takers had handed out along with the program when we entered the stands. There were pictures of several Cincinnati players, some of them wearing caps with the letter C encircled on their front. This seemed to be a cap no longer worn by the Reds, and I recalled that our Van Lear town team once had caps like that. When I mentioned this to Dad, he said that they wore those after his brother Everett played. Then he said, "Did you know that a team of Big Sandy all stars beat the Reds in an exhibition game at Louisa back in the twenties?"

A 1926-era Van Lear baseball team sporting uniforms with the Consol logo "C" on their caps.

When I said that I didn't know that, he said, "Everett played in that game, along with Bob Jasper, Bitty Beers, and Doctor Paul Hall." Dad told me this with a bit of pride in his voice, as he was very fond of his brother Everett, who was called "Sook" by his close friends. I asked if Fred Vinson played on that team, but he said he didn't know about that.

One of Van Lear's better town baseball teams. Front row, left to right, Elbert "Bitty" Beers (c), Bob Jasper (p), Conrad Kirk (3b), Ganey Newman (2b), and Homer Robinson (2b). Back row, team manager Emmett Lambert, Roy Murray (rf), Everett "Sook" Vaughan (p), Carl Preston (cf), Tom Blair (lf), Clyde Preston (1b), and Paul B. Hall (ss). This team won most of its contests in 1920, including an exhibition game victory over the Cincinnati Reds at Louisa, and a 7 - 2 win over a Huntington, West Virginia, team.

My heart sank when I looked at the National League team standings. The two hot teams were the Saint Louis Cardinals and the Chicago Cubs. The Reds were in seventh place, one notch above the bottom, and I wondered if their team had been that awful when the Big Sandy All Stars beat them. The Cardinals were now known as the Gashouse Gang—don't ask me why—and some of the men in our part of the bleachers were saying that they were the team to beat for the National League Pennant. Two of their standouts were the brothers Paul and Dizzy Dean, both fastball pitchers. The Reds had Paul Derringer and Dazzy Vance, but Vance was now in his forties, and even I knew that was old for a big league pitcher. They also had another right-handed starter named Benny Frey, but not much else in the way of pitchers. The Cards had players like Rip Collins and Leo Durocher, who had been traded to the St. Louis team for Derringer, and their manager, Frankie Frisch, was playing second base. I began to search the field, looking for my hero, Pepper Martin. The *Ashland Daily Independent* had run a story that said Pepper was paid over eight thousand dollars a year, more than four times what a coal miner made. When I mentioned this to Dad, he said that Babe Ruth earned more than fifty thousand dollars a year, an unimaginable sum of money. I shut up about Pepper Martin when he told me this, and tried hard to see who was playing third base for the Cards. I could see that someone was playing third base, but it could be anybody. We were sitting too far away to make out facial features. As the game got underway, the public address announcer told us that Paul Derringer would be on the mound for the Reds, and some new rookie would pitch for the Cards. We wouldn't see the Reds' ace, old dependable Dazzy Vance, or either of the Cards' marvels from Arkansas, the Dean brothers. I scanned the newsletter once more and learned that Derringer was a Kentucky boy, born in 1906 at Springfield.

Because we passed up the forty-cent bean soup at the train station and I had only eaten a candy bar since leaving home, Dad hailed the concessionaire and bought us hot dogs and sodas. Then we settled back to enjoy the game as the organ player finished the national anthem and began blasting forth with "Take Me Out To The Ballgame."

Both teams had at each other for four and a half innings, with neither one looking all that major league. Of course, we were so far out in right field that the finer points of play occurred without our having any real firsthand knowledge of them. I was painfully aware of our distance from the action, being accustomed to the intimacy of our small ball park back in Van Lear where you could sit right behind the screen in back of the catcher and see every pitch, but I never once thought to complain about this to Dad, as this was something kids just didn't do, especially after being treated to a special trip like this.

Strangely, perhaps because of our walk through colored town, I begin to wonder why there were no black athletes playing in these games. Where were Josh Gibson and others like him, all major-league caliber baseball players. And then I remember. They are in a separate Negro league of their own, sometimes playing in Ashland and other larger and mid-sized towns all over America, often opposing teams made up of white players, but never playing *with* white players, and again I wonder why, but I don't ask anyone about this. After all, I'm just a young kid, and I know my place.

The first game was a real pitchers' duel. By the time the final out is made I have a new hero named Frank McCormick, who came in as a pinch hitter and hit the game's only homer to win the contest for Cincinnati.

During the break between games, I listen to the men talk about their favorite baseball players. One of Dad's friends has very little good to say about the Cincinnati Reds. "Just look at 'em, lucky boobs," he says, "and name one guy who'll lead in any category in the National League this year."

Everyone is silent, except Dad, who speaks up for one Red. "Derringer," he says, without hesitation. "Paul Derringer could play for anybody."

The friend shrugs agreeably, and then says, "Name another."

"Lombardi," Dad says. And that's where they left it.

I look at my copy of the newsletter, trying hard to come up with another Red worthy of mention. Hafey, Koenig, Slade–all of them are batting well below three hundred. The second game has begun. Another pitcher's duel, it drags on as I concentrate on the slick fielding of Joe Medwick, the Cards' outfielder they call "Ducky." The game ends, finally, with the Cards in the lead. We're ready to go home, back up Big Sandy.

Instead of walking back to the train terminal, we share a taxi with two other people. The return trip late that night and into the early Monday morning hours is anticlimactic. What a day it has been! Two big-league baseball games, the train trip, and the chance to talk with Dad about so many things. Maybe *that* was the best part of all. I put my flop-eared cap and the Ashland book in a paper sack, and rest my head upon it. Too tired to read, I decide to adopt the Cardinals as my team, leaving the Reds for Richard, and then I fall asleep, dreaming all the while of the great baseball players I have seen, and of my beloved hills back home.

The stop at Vanceburg awakens me, and I rub the sleep from my eyes and open the window and stare out onto the darkened station platform, but only for a second. Something soft and squishy hits me smack dab in the kisser, and I draw my head back inside and rub my stinging face. When I look at my hand it is covered with red watermelon juice, and I quickly wipe it away and look nervously around the coach to see if anyone has seen this, but no one has, and I vow not to mention it to anyone. Satisfied that I have not been seriously injured, I go to the washroom, wash off the watermelon pulp, and return to my seat where I soon drift off to sleep once again.

The lonesome train whistle awakens me, and I glance outside.

The C&O rail passenger station at Ashland, much as it must have looked late that Sunday night in July 1934, when our baseball excursion train returned from Cincinnati.

In the early morning hours a haze hangs over the low valleys, obscuring the peaks and ridges as it often does in these parts. The moon shines through, but dimly. On this summer morning it is a blue moon, a once-in-a-great-while moon. The moon and haze bathe everything in a pale, ethereal blue, adding to the feeling of isolation and solitude, as only a moon over Kentucky can do, and the sight of that moon fills me with a strange foreboding. But that feeling is short-lived as I doze off once more. Then, almost before I know it, the conductor has announced our station, but I don't hear his call as we approach West Van Lear. Dad rouses me, and I reach for the sack containing my precious book. We step off the train, the narrow cinder path faintly visible in the morning haze. We board the waiting bus for the final three miles up Miller's Creek. It has been a good, but long and tiring day. Soon Dad will return to the mines, and I will join Richard and Billy and play in the hills once more, or play baseball, or perhaps watch Big John spar. It is summer-lovely, carefree, glorious summer!

Central Van Lear. My good friend, Richard Sparks (PHS 1944), and his family lived in the second house at the right in the foreground. The main mule barn is near the center, with the central company store above it, and the recreation building and houses along Silk Stocking Row at the upper right. The Consol office building is at the upper left.

Chapter Two
A Van Lear Boyhood

Blessings on thee, little man,
barefoot boy, with cheeks of tan.

—*Whittier*

It was ten o'clock the next morning when Bobby and Earl knocked on the back door of our house. Our house was just a small cottage, not one of the two-story houses like the house Richard and his folks lived in. I slept in a tiny room, off the living room and kitchen, and I could hear my mother tell them she'd rather not wake me yet, but I got up anyway when I heard them, and after I pulled on my overalls and gulped down some corn flakes and milk, with Mom standing there telling me not to eat so fast, I bolted out the door. When I saw the look on Bobby and Earl's faces, I realized that because I had been on the Cincinnati baseball excursion I was now a celebrity in a minor-league sort of way. I could tell by the way they acted that they wanted to know all about the trip and the games.

Richard had been sent up to the commissary by his mother. After we found him, Billy joined us, and then there were five of us traipsing along the main road, past the old mule barn and brightly painted company houses, our feet scarcely touching the ground, the sun high in the sky, another beautiful July day. We decided that if we found Tommy, maybe we should round up three other guys and challenge the River Rats to a baseball game. My trip to see the Reds and Cards had really motivated all of the guys, even Earl, who was sometimes lazy and hard to arouse, and I could see that they were really curious to know all about the games, even old Earl, but I kept putting them off, saving the story for later.

After we found Tommy and Johnny, who were hanging out at the pool room, I just sort of swaggered along for a ways, still not saying anything. I didn't have to wait long before Bobby piped up and asked, "What was Derringer's best pitch?" Right away I said that it was his fast ball. Actually from where we had sat way out in the Crosley Field bleachers I hadn't been able to tell what any of the pitches were, but my answer must have sounded reasonable.

"Yeh, that was it," I allowed, feeling that special glow from having been there. "His fast ball was his best one," I said confidently, and no one found fault with my answer. After all, the guys had only heard the radio broadcast.

Billy and Earl wanted to know about how Van Lear players would stack up against the Reds. "Just as good," I told them without even hesitating.

Earl, who had a high-pitched kind of voice, questioned this. "Ah come on, Spud," he said, "you don't really believe that, do you?"

I looked old Earl square in the eye, and then I said, "Maybe Snail is even better."

Snail was James Estill Lambert, whose nickname was Snail, one of the guys who played on the town team. He could really rare back and throw the old horsehide, especially the curve ball.

On our way back to Richard's house we ran into Pete, and it only took us a minute to ask him to join us. Billy had some reservations about asking him, since Pete lived near Number One mine, between us and Bradley Crossing, but when he remembered that Pete was a slick fielder and hitter, he agreed that it would be okay. We waited outside while Richard took the bag of groceries in to his mother, and then we continued on our way to the river.

As we walked along, I told the guys other things about the Reds' and Cards' game, but I didn't tell them about the walk through colored town, where I had been really scared, something I hadn't said anything about even to my dad. I didn't tell them about getting hit in the face with the water melon rind either, but I did tell them about the fancy club car, and seeing the congressman and all the other high-falutin' brass and big shots, and I could tell they were all really impressed with this and the other stuff I told them. I swaggered along big time, feeling my oats, as they say.

By the time we reached the carpentry shop, Oren had joined us, and when he said he would play in the outfield we had the necessary nine players, but then we ran into Eddie who was almost as good a player as Pete, so we asked him to come with us too. Johnny could sit on the bench and be a substitute. A good team always needed a good substitute, we told him, and so, with Tommy, Pete, and Eddie on our side, we were feeling pretty good as we went on our merry way, with me retelling my story for the latecomers.

All of us boys were, for the most part, good friends. We had a good life and we knew it, even when the grown-ups were in charge, which was practically all of the time, but not on this particular day. Including Pete on our team was something of a departure from the norm, but then Eddie wasn't one of our regular gang either, since he was visiting from Oil Springs, and neither was Tommy, but there was no telling who the river bunch would drag out to play on their team, maybe guys from West Van Lear Junction or even Paintsville.

Our friends and playmates were mostly the guys who lived in our part of town. Van Lear's western boundary begins a few miles east of Paintsville. In fact, the two city limits are separated mostly by West Van Lear Junction. That's where the Miller's Creek Railroad from Van Lear joins the main C&O line, the place where Dad and I boarded the excursion train yesterday, which now seemed like a week or more ago.

Just east of West Van Lear Junction is the westernmost part of Van Lear, which everyone referred to as the River. Each of the town's neighborhoods had its set of young boys and each neighborhood had its neighborhood team, one for every sport. The players remained pretty much the same, although we sometimes borrowed players from each other, and each sport had its season. If you begin

The steam-powered electric plant at the river, source of electricity for Van Lear and, for a time, the city of Paintsville. The main line of the C&O Railroad is just beyond the tree line in the foggy distance. After the water-cooling pond at the left was removed, the River Rats sometimes played baseball and football on the field that replaced it. The Barnyard Gang played the River Rats to a scoreless tie in the flat space between rows of company houses in 1934. There were no extra innings that day.

at the western edge of town, there were the West Van Lear Junctioneers and the River Rats. Next, heading east, were the Bradley Crossing Gang, who had the only easy access to the football field. Everyone else had to walk from one to three miles to use its facilities. Bradley Crossing had been unofficially given that name in honor of locomotive engineer Will Bradley, who brought the first steam locomotive from Parkersburg, West Virginia, and who still piloted the coal trains into and out of Van Lear. The Bradley Crossing bunch included Richard Adams, Marcus and Charles Spears, Billy and Earl Rucker, Junior Adams, Robert Jasper, and one or more of the Fishers, Conleys, Pelphreys, and Campbells, and maybe even Buddy Caudill or a Wells or Webb or two.

At midtown, Richard, Johnny, James, Bobby, Billy, Tommy, Dick, Howard Russell, and I were the Barnyard Gang, since we played in the open space near the old mule barn. Pete and his brothers, and

Oakley and Spider Webb sometimes had their own team, but today Pete was one of us. Then there was Silk Stocking Row next to the clubhouse and recreation building, across from the main store, community house, and office building. The clubhouse was where all the visiting dignitaries from the Consol home office stayed when they were in town, and it was really nice. There was a big dining room and a lounge, which they sometimes made into a ballroom, where they had special dances. They even let the high school have their proms there. Like I've been trying to tell you, Van Lear was really nice, far nicer than a lot of the coal towns. In fact, it really didn't deserve to be called a coal camp, which is what they called some of the other company-owned mining towns.

The Packs, Kellys, Youngs, Wills, and Rices usually played with a group of boys from Sorghum or Possum Holler. While I'm think-

Silva Lyon and Hampton Kemper (both VLHS 1925) knew these Van Lear homes as the "boardwalk houses" in 1918, although when this photo was taken, neither the boardwalk nor the road had been completed. The Methodist Church is seen in the distance. Not visible at the right were the homes and playground of the Bradley Crossing Gang.

This photo was made after a snowfall, looking west along the railroad toward the mule barn, where our Barnyard Gang played sandlot baseball, basketball, and football games.

An early photo of the club house and recreation building. Unmarried faculty members and visiting company officials "boarded" at the club house. The "Rec" or "Fountain" building housed a soda fountain, pool hall, beauty parlor, and a theater where first-run movies and occasional big bands and other such shows were featured. Sorghum Holler is to the left and Possum Holler, not visible, to the right

ing of it, that's the way we said that word—not hollow—although that is the way it's spelled. Possum Holler is where the Bowlings lived, and they almost had enough guys our age to make up their own teams, but, whenever we could, Richard and I would borrow any one of them because they were all good athletes, besides being good musicians. The Butcher boys lived and played over on Buffalo, across from the Number Five mine, which was now the main mine opening and the town's principal source of employment. Richard and I always hated to play at Number Five, partly because there were lots of cinders on their playing field, and if you fell you usually got a lot of nicks and scratches, and there was this big slate dump that was always burning and giving off a sulfur-like smoke that really stunk. The main reason we didn't like to play them was they always beat us, no matter what the sport was. The Number Five team usually had Tommy, Tony, Frankie, John, Leo, and some of the Butcher boys, and they were *really* good players.

The store just to the west of Mine No. 155 and Butcher Holler. Loretta Lynn's brother Herman now owns this property, but in the 1930s it was owned and operated by Consol; we would visit it to refresh ourselves with a peach Nehi after a spirited baseball game with the No. 5 gang.

Our town of Van Lear was nearly five miles long, and all of us boys got around either on foot or on bicycles. On this particular Monday we were all afoot since Billy had been grounded for some minor infraction of the rules at his house, and we were trying to sneak him outside his premises without his being missed, so we agreed to leave the bikes at home, which made his folks think we were still there, playing somewhere near their house. We did things like that a lot back then, and at the time we didn't think our moms ever caught on to us, but now that I think of it they may have known about some of our shenanigans and just turned the other way.

On the way to the river we decided if we couldn't get a baseball game with the River crowd, we could always go swimming, and our parents would never be the wiser. We sometimes did this, and, in fact, that's how most of us learned to swim in the backwater at the mouth of Millers Creek when the river was flooded. If our moms had known about that at the time, they would have had a hissy-fit or worse. As we trudged along, baseball gloves dangling from bats slung over our shoulders, Tommy regaled us with wild tales about some of the things the older men had told him on one of their baseball trips. Tommy was such a good player, some of the men had taken him and Tony under their wings, so to speak, and let them go on some of their baseball trips with them.

We had to make a special stop to get permission for Pete to play. To get his mom to let him go with us, we had to agree to come back no later than three o'clock. That's when his dad was due home, and Pete had to help him gather roasting ears from their garden. Pete said that was okay, he would do that, and so we then headed for the river, walking along like a ragtag kid baseball team, although we didn't feel like just any old pickup team. We always proudly called ourselves the Barnyard Gang, and now we had three of the best players in Van Lear with old Tommy, Pete, and Eddie. With them playing for us, we shouldn't have any trouble beating the River Rats.

Most of the River bunch had been lying around with nothing much to do that day, so they rounded up their team and the game began soon after we got there. We should have objected to their using Perry McCloud from West Van Lear Junction, but we didn't, since we had three players who lived outside our neighborhood.

When their pitcher got our side out, three in a row with no trouble, we visitors knew we were in for a rough game. As it turned out, the game was destined to set some kind of record as the shortest one we ever played and our only scoreless tie. Here's what happened: Earl pitched, Tommy caught, and I played first base. Pete was on second, Richard on third, and Billy was the shortstop. Oren, Eddie, and Bobby made up the outfield, with Johnny in reserve. The game started off with what the sportswriters might refer to as a "pitchers' duel," just like the Reds and Cards, with neither side hitting a ball out of the infield. Their pitcher was almost as good as Earl. The game was still scoreless when Earl walked a batter in the third inning. Then, with two out, the runner took off from first base, and Tommy pegged the ball to Pete who was covering second. Mr. Finley, who had agreed to be the umpire, called the runner safe. How he could see all the way from home to second was something Earl questioned. The play was close. Earl walked right up to the ump and, in that high-pitched voice of his, told him he was blind as a bat, but then the umpire just stared him down and stood his ground. Earl didn't say any more, but just spit like he was chewing tobacco, and stared back. He finally accepted the umpire's decision, and Pete walked back to the mound with him, and said something to him, then all of us went back to our regular positions.

Earl got his sign from Tommy and stretched, holding the runner at second base. The runner took a cautious lead off second. Pete then walked over to the man on second, tagged him on the butt with the ball, and held the ball up in the air for the ump to see. The umpire called the runner out, and all hell broke loose.

The river boys didn't take too kindly to the hidden ball trick. As it turned out, we were lucky to get out of there without any serious personal injuries. Although Oren would later claim that he had wanted to stand his ground and fight, the truth is he ran like a demon possessed, just like the rest of us. Earl's excuse was that we were outnumbered in foreign territory and, besides, the sun was really getting hot, and Pete had to get on back home to help his dad gather and shuck corn.

With nothing else to do when we got back home, Richard and I decided to work on the baseball board game we started to make a week ago. Richard's dad had given him a really neat wooden box, and the two of us were convinced that this one would be the ultimate baseball board game. We even speculated if this game turned out the way we planned it, we might just market it under the trade name, "The Vaughan-Sparks Gee-Whiz Baseball Game," or something of that sort. The more we thought and talked about it, the mightier and wilder our imaginations. It could even be good enough to be offered as a premium on one of the radio shows, like "Jack Armstrong" or "Little Orphan Annie," we decided. Richard and I were always imagining some such enterprise, complete with trademarks and all. Once we imagineered a new automobile that we would one day market through our own company, AMNAT, short for "American National." Our first model was to be a dazzling new coupe that we planned to call "The Demoniac." But that project had been put on hold when baseball season came.

For the "Gee-Whiz Baseball Game," we first marked off a diamond and outfield, and then we borrowed a small hand-drill and drilled holes to make pockets where the marbles could land without dropping through, and we labeled them with black ink to indicate an out, a single, a double, triple, or homer. To the left and right of the foul lines we made boxed-in areas ringed by small nails, and we then marked them to represent foul balls or, behind homeplate, strikes. The homerun area was the most difficult to reach since it was surrounded by a barricade of nails and holes representing fly balls that had been caught by fleet-footed outfielders. We painted the field's surface green, which we then striped with white paint along the foul lines and down the base lines. Richard whittled a wooden bat and attached it to a rubber band, and we then drilled a small hole through its base and attached it to the bottom of the board. The free end of the rubber band was fixed to a nail near shortstop, and a strong cord was tied to the bat to provide a kind of trigger-release. Balls were marbles, which we would drop, one at a time, down a runway through a hole near the centerfield fence. The pitcher tried to catch the batter off-guard and vary his timing of his deliveries to make it more difficult for the batter to hit the ball. The batter, in turn, tried to time his release of the spring-loaded bat to make the best possible contact with the ball.

That evening after supper we put the ball game on hold, and Richard and I went over to the Number One bathhouse to see Big John spar. There were only a dozen or so black people then living in Van Lear, and Big John was one of them, and the only one we had ever seen in midtown. The reason we knew about the sparring match was because Mack Mckinney's pretty daughter had told us what her dad was planning to do.

When we got there we found this white guy punching away at a big canvas bag, so we sat down on the concrete floor and watched. The white guy was someone whose nickname was Huffy, and he didn't say a thing when he saw us, but just kept on punching. Richard whispered to me that he had heard that Huffy was probably the best athlete in all of Johnson County. Huffy, stripped to the waist and wearing old dungaree pants and tennis shoes, finally stopped punching the bag and came over to where we sat. Wiping the sweat from his face with one of his boxing gloves, he hailed us, "Hey, boys. How you doin'?" he asked, and we just sat there, sort of honored that this older guy would even speak to us like that.

Just then, Mack McKinney came in with Big John, followed by Billy, who ran over to Richard and me and squatted next to us on the cement floor. Mack was the only one that we knew in Van Lear who had ever boxed, and Big John had said he would like to learn that sport too. Huffy was the guy Mack had found to spar with John.

"Hi, guys," Billy said, and we howdied with Billy, and watched

The No. 151 mine area c. 1914, before all of the houses were completed. The No. 151 mine tipple is shown in the distance, with the bathhouse (the white building in the center near the tipple) where Richard and I witnessed the sparring session. Other structures include maintenance buildings and houses near Bradley Crossing.

as Big John stripped to the waist and donned his gloves. Mack, meanwhile, hung a whistle over his neck, rolled up the sleeves of his sweatshirt, turned his billed baseball cap facing backwards, and began marking off a square on the floor with a piece of chalk. When he finished doing this he motioned for John and Huffy.

"Now, boys," Mack said, "when I blow this whistle, it means break clean and stop punching. Ya' hear?" Both men nodded and the sparring session began.

Huffy was well-built, but Big John was even better-built, with huge biceps and a neck maybe twice the size of Huffy's, but it was obvious from the start that old Huffy knew some tricks that John had never learned, like how to cover up with his gloves, feint with both hands, and then step in and nail him one, which he did soon after the session began. This caught Big John by surprise, and he sort of turned his head aside, and that's when Huffy caught him with another overhand right. Mack McKinney blew his whistle, and pushed the two men apart.

"Boys," Mack said, and then he started over. "Men," he began again, this time emphasizing men, "this is a sparring match, see? So, I'll stop you both from time to time to explain something. Now, John, you must not look away. Do you see what Huffy is doin'?"

The big guy nodded and said, "Yeh, he's hittin' me in the face every time."

"Okay," Mack said. "Right. Now, what is he doin' that makes it possible for him to hit you in the face?"

"Well," John said hesitantly, not sure how to say it. "He jumps around and acts like he's punchin', and I duck, and that's when he lets me have one right in the kisser."

"That's right," Mack said, laughing as he said it, and then all of us laughed too. "Now, what I want you to do," Mack said, "is the same thing Huffy is doing. Bob and weave and feint with your left and wait for an opening, and then you let him have it right back. Okay?" Big John nodded, Mack blew his whistle, and the two men started in again.

Huffy began to bob and weave and feint with his left and then, when he started to jab with his left, John stepped back out of the way so that Huffy's left jab missed, and when it did, Big John let fly with a hard overhand right that landed over Huffy's left ear, sending him reeling backward, flat of his back. Mack blew his whistle, and ran over to help Huffy back on his feet.

After Huffy shook off the effects of John's blow, Mack asked him if he was okay, and then he walked over to John and said, "That's the way to do it, John. Keep that up and you could be a pro some day." Then, turning back to Huffy, he said, "Huffy, you've got to keep your guard up. Your feint was okay, but you've got to still keep your guard up. Now, gents, let's have at it again."

The two went after each other pretty good for a full two minutes, and then Mack blew his whistle once more, and you could see that both men were glad to have a time-out. Huffy was wringing wet with sweat and so was Big John, and both men were pretty winded, so they sat down together on one of the bathhouse benches, and Mack motioned for one of us to get the water bucket, which Billy did, since he was sitting nearest it. Not sure who he should hand it to, Billy looked at both men, and then sat the water bucket and a cup in front of Huffy.

Huffy dipped the cup into the water, and started to drink from it, but then he thought better of it, and handed his cup to Big John and said simply, "Here, John."

The big guy hesitated, then took the cup of water and, with a broad smile on his face, said, "Thanks, man."

Richard, Billy, and I looked all around the bath house, inspecting it, and noticing all the stuff for the first time. We had heard about it, but had never been inside it. The bath house was a big old building with a high ceiling. Overhead were a hundred or more wire baskets, each attached to a chain that dangled down to within about six feet of the floor. As I stood there gazing up at the baskets, I could see that some were empty, while others either contained clean street clothes, or grimy work clothes. The street clothes belonged to the few who were still in the mines, doing maintenance work. There was one chain and basket for each miner, and each man had his own check number and a padlock to keep others from using his chain hoist and getting into his basket and messing with his clothing and personal stuff, like watches and rings and things. One whole end of the building was partitioned off with a wall full of shower heads, and a floor with water drains. The part of the building nearest the entrance had no overhead chains, and this was where Mack McKinney had marked off the sparring ring. The whole place was dank and smelled of mildew, coal dust, and workers' sweat.

Mack motioned John and Huffy to start in again, and we watched the sparring session for another ten minutes, listening intently to the instructions Mack gave each fighter, and noticing the improvements in both men as they learned from experience and Mack's advice. At last, Mack blew his whistle and said, "Okay, men, that's it. You both had a good workout. Take a shower. We'll do it again some other time." When I got home that evening I made sure I didn't say anything about where I had been. Dad wouldn't have liked it. He called boxing a "brute sport."

The next afternoon, I rummaged through a dungaree pocket and found a scrip nickel. These were sort of gold-colored coins with the Consolidation Coal Company name stamped on them. Consol issued scrip money to their miners if they wanted to draw some of their pay before payday. Unlike some of the other coal companies, who paid their miners only in scrip that had to be spent at their stores, Consol paid off in U.S. currency, providing the miner waited until pay day. Consol issued scrip coins in pennies, which were octagon-shaped coppers, goldish nickels, thin dimes, quarters, half-

The fountain room at the recreation building. Neither the pool room nor the candy counters where I discovered "The Big Rock Candy Mountain" are visible here.

dollars, and big, wagon-wheel silver dollars. A 1934 scrip or silver dollar would be worth $20 to $30 or more today.

After supper, I managed to slip off to the Fountain—that's what most of us called the recreation building—where I spent my nickel on a candy bar. Then I went into the pool room, where I knew I would most likely find my brother George. Sure enough, there he was, playing pool with his friends, Harold Rucker and Erwin Brown. I eased up onto the bench, and sat there a long time, just watching them play. All three of them were good players, and sometimes my brother George was really good. That evening, they were playing eight-ball for a dollar a game, and George had just raked in the three big scrip dollars after winning the last game. He broke the next rack, and sat down for a moment right beside me, and that's when I asked him for some money to buy candy. He looked at me, handed me a scrip dollar, and went back to playing. I immediately got up from my seat, and went into the adjoining fountain room.

This photo shows Demart Bowling working behind the counter at a restored "Ickie's" in the basement of the old Consol office building, some sixty-eight years after my big candy purchase from the original Richard "Ickie" Wetzel at the Fountain in 1934.

Ickie Wetzel looked at me kind of strangely when I handed him the scrip dollar. Then he asked me what I wanted, and I started pointing to different kinds of candy displayed under the glass-topped showcase. "How much?" Ickie asked.

I looked back at him, and said, "All of it." He really had a funny look on his face when I said that. Most of the candy was priced at maybe a dime a pound or less. He asked me again, how much, and I answered him the same, all of it, and he grinned and started loading up a big brown sack with all the different kinds of candy in the showcase. Just when I thought that I had bought all the dollar would buy, he indicated that I had more coming, and so I pointed to other candy, and still more and more until, at long last, he said that's it, and I looked at the huge bag of candy and thought that I had found The Big Rock Candy Mountain.

When I reentered the poolroom, and reclaimed my perch on the onlookers' bench, everyone noticed that I was carrying this huge brown bag, which must have contained from ten to twelve pounds of candy. I reached into the sack, and began eating candy, thinking how lucky I was, what with Dad taking me on that special baseball excursion, and now my brother buying me all this candy! But then, a moment later, George exploded my little bubble when he asked me for his change.

I shook my head and told him there wasn't any change, and an odd sort of expression came over his face. When he realized that I had spent the whole dollar, his face began to turn red, and he said, "Well, don't just sit there. Pass it around." Reluctantly, I climbed down from my perch on the bench and did as I was told, my momentary dream of having all the candy I could eat evaporating before my very eyes.

A couple of days later, Walter and Billy visited Richard and me and saw the baseball game we were making, and they were so impressed they went back to Walter's house and made one of their own and began to practice with it, but ours was still the best, and for the next two days we four boys crawled under Richard's house, where it was at least ten degrees cooler, and there in that dark and dusty cavern, we pulled off our shoes and had a whole series of games between Walter and Billy's Cubs, and mine and Richard's Cardinals, complete with scorecards, names of players, their batting averages, the whole bit. In case you're wondering why Richard and I opted for the Cardinals, it was because the Reds had dropped all the way down to last place, and the Cards were on a roll, well on their way to a National League pennant.

Our games on our homemade baseball box were better than pinball, we all agreed and, besides, none of us had nickels to drop into pinball machines. We were halfway through the second day's round of games when Old Lucky, my black fox terrier, started acting kind of strange. We looked outside and could see that a summer rainstorm had come up and cooled things down, and so, then and there and without anyone saying a word, we got out our steel hoops, which we had salvaged from some old barrels over at the Number One Mine, and we went off like demons possessed, rolling the hoops down Main Street, with Old Lucky in close pursuit, yapping at our heels. Bobby joined us when he saw how much fun we were having, but hoop rolling didn't last long, and we decided to get out our carts and have a race.

Our carts were homemade affairs, nothing like the slick jobs that competed in the National Soap Box Derby at Akron up in Ohio. The best that most Van Lear boys could manage was four wheels, two axles, and enough boards and nails to hammer a rolling frame together. Some were lucky enough to find two steel axles, while the rest settled for broom sticks. Our raceway was the steep and dangerous gravel alley above our house, which ended up crossing the main road. Our parents didn't much like this amusement, but back in the 1930s there wasn't much in the way of automobile traffic in Van Lear. On this particular outing, I broke a broomstick axle the first time down the hill, and that ended the day's cart race. We returned to Richard's house and sat on the front stoop and tried to decide what we should do next.

A lot of the games we played just seemed to appear out of nowhere. Take the game we called "Elephant," for instance. To play Elephant, you needed at least six players on each side. One team was the elephant, which consisted of a postman, who stood upright with one leg extended. Around this leg, the front man locked his arms and assumed a bent-over posture with each of the remaining men also bent over, one behind the other, leaving the end man's rump exposed. The other team ran, one at a time, and jumped astride the elephant, each man attempting to leap as far ahead as possible toward the postman, without letting his feet touch the ground. If you could get all of the members of your team onto the back of the elephant without anyone's feet touching the ground, you then had the right to shake the elephant until it collapsed, in which case you could rise up and do it all over again. Should any team member allow his feet to touch the ground, that team then became the elephant and the other team got a whack at you.

Another game requiring a certain amount of gymnastic ability was called "Tumblebug." I think the name came from those little summer bugs that made a living rolling balls of manure, which Billy said they stored for their families to eat during the long winter months. For this game you needed two teams of four members each. The "down" team assumed a bent-over posture with two side-men, their rumps backed up to each other, and two end-men with their heads stuck under these rumps and their arms locked about the side-men's legs. Members of the other "up" team then took turns doing running leaps and flips by placing their hands on the front rump, flipping or somersaulting in the air, landing back-to-back on the backside of the rearmost rump, and bouncing off without falling to earth. The rules for Tumblebug were similar to those for Elephant in that as long as your team members could perform these flips without stepping on an opponent's foot or falling to the ground, you could continue this routine, over and over. Charles Bowling and Lawrence Young were especially adept at this sport, having learned to flip high in the air and come down with considerable force while avoiding a foul. One of my classmates, who shall be nameless, took a cheap shot one day, and kicked me in the rear when I was bent over as the end-man. I limped around for days, lucky to escape with only enlarged veins in the nether regions, and I'm sure my nasal twang rose an octave or two after that incident.

If these games seem potentially dangerous, then consider what our parents would have done had they been aware of what went on within the sheltering confines of the banks of Miller's Creek, where we would sometimes go to practice archery. The willows that grew along the stream provided an ample source of material for bows, strong twine or staging from the store made fine bowstrings, and light and straight ash gave us what we needed for arrows. It was the arrows that turned us into potential killers since we tipped them with sharpened horseshoe nails. One day Bud lodged an arrow in Jackie Roger's skull. My God! He had wounded the mine inspector's son! All of us immediately abandoned this particular activity in favor of rubber guns. Ammunition consisted of long pieces of rubber innertubing which were looped across the end of the gun. The two loose ends were then stretched to the trigger where they were held in place until ready to be fired by a spring-loaded clothespin. Although rubber guns could cause a painful blister when fired at close range, they weren't nearly as dangerous as arrows tipped with horseshoe nails.

Most Van Lear boys owned BB guns at one time or another, and these too could be quite dangerous. One day George Anderson, Junior, was resting the tip of his left index finger on the barrel of his brother Earl's Daisy air rifle when something or someone tripped the trigger. Earl's gun wasn't just your ordinary BB gun. It was one you could pump up with its own self-contained air pump, and this time it had been pumped up until you could probably kill a person with it if you hit him in the right place. The BB went right through the skin and lodged in Junior's finger. After he went off to the company doctor to get the BB removed, Richard and I spent the rest of that day and most of the next hiding out, hoping the police wouldn't find us and take us into custody. Neither of us knew which of us had tripped the trigger, but since George Junior's sister, Ethel, would one day be our fifth-grade teacher, we were both especially wary of running into any of the Andersons for the rest of that summer.

When we rode the train down to Ashland the next week, I was relieved to learn that my mother and dad apparently knew nothing about the BB gun incident, and I was free to run through the hills and along the creeks with Cousins Charles and Richard Vaughan. Grandma Lynk lived at Kilgore, the little settlement I told you about earlier. She lived there alone with her son Joe and Joe's wife, Aunt Clara. Her husband, Granddad John Lynk, had died some years earlier. Some of Dad's kin didn't like Kilgore, and they had moved on, but Mom's father settled on that little hamlet as the place to set up his blacksmith shop, and provide his ironmonger's services to the coal and iron trade that had been established in Boyd and Carter County, Kentucky. His old blacksmith shop was still standing, down the lane behind the Barrett's big house. Uncle Charley Barrett not only had the finest home there, but also the biggest store building. Charles and Richard Vaughan's mother, Aunt Mary, was Uncle Charley and Aunt May Barrett's daughter. Aunt Mary had married Dad's brother Wayne, who had died in a slate fall in a mine over in West Virginia.

My father, Jim Vaughan, at the left, with Avery Burton and Avery Burton, Junior, at Kilgore, Boyd County, Kentucky, around 1925. My cousins Junior Burton and Charles and Richard Vaughan and I watched Uncle Charley Barrett's big store burn to the ground there late one night some nine years later.

The morning after we arrived in Kilgore, I climbed out of the feather bed, found Aunt Mary's nephew Junior Burton, who was hanging out at Tid Safert's store, and, together with Charles and Richard, went fishing in Williams Creek. The only thing we caught that day was a big mud turtle, which we brought back to Aunt Mary. When we asked her to cook it for us, she agreed only after we said we would clean it, which we did. We had been told that a turtle had six different flavors, including chicken, but it didn't taste like any of them.

The next day, Mom's older sister, Aunt Mayme, and her husband, Uncle Bill Howell, came to visit Grandma Lynk. Charles and I found some hickory limbs, and Uncle Bill helped us make bows and arrows.

That evening after Aunt Stella Burton played some pieces on Grandma's pump organ, I mentioned the wart on my right hand, and Aunt Stella and the other ladies told me I should visit Mrs. Black, a widow woman, who could cast spells on warts. After they told me where to find her, Mom gave me a quarter to give to Mrs. Black, and I set out walking up the road. It was getting late in the evening when I crossed over a footbridge, and found the place where the spellcaster lived. With some forebodings, I knocked on her door. When she called out from within, I told the wizened little lady why I was there, entered her house and sat by her side while she held my right hand, told me to close my eyes, and then muttered some words. "That's it," she said.

That night we were all awakened by the smell of smoke, the sound of a crackling fire, and a bright orange glow lighting up the sky. When we looked outside, Charlie Barrett's big store building was ablaze. Throwing on our clothes, all of us rushed outside, and the men started forming a bucket brigade. Dad even went inside the flaming building to try to save some of the Barrett's chickens, while Mom stood outside yelling at him to get out, which he did just before the whole structure came tumbling down.

The next morning Charles and Richard and I picked through

the smoldering debris, salvaging hard candy that hadn't burned, even though it now had a smoky taste to it. Dad decided that he needed to go back to Van Lear, while Mom said she wanted to stay a few days longer, and they agreed that Dad would take me back with him. But I was having such a good time, I thought up a way to stay. When no one was looking, I took my shoes and hid them back of Grandma's house, near a rain barrel. Without shoes, I reasoned, I wouldn't have to go with Dad. Imagine my surprise when I learned that Mom and Aunt Mayme had both seen me hiding the shoes, and when it came time to go, they handed them to me.

I loved those visits, even the dark nights when I would sit there in the old Lynk house in the glow of the kerosene lamps, listening to the old folks tell their stories, reveling in the gentle warmth generated by Grandma Lynk, now blinded with a milky film over her eyes, sometimes smoking a clay pipe, and occasionally muttering to herself in her native German, which she had refused to allow her children to learn. Once, during a lull in the conversation, I looked down at my hand and noticed that the wart was still there. This set the adults to offering advice on what I could do to remove the wretched thing.

"Mrs. Black's spell usually works," Aunt Clara said.

"Milkweed," Aunt Mayme offered. "We used to use milkweed juice for warts. Just rubbed it on, and soon the wart was gone."

"Or dandelions," Mom suggested. "I seem to remember rubbing them with dandelions."

"That sounds like something old Bowman would say," Aunt Mayme said, laughing at her younger sister's suggestion.

"Fan loved old Bowman's candy," Grandma added, and everyone laughed long and hard when she said it. Fan was my mother's nickname. Bowman was an old man who lived alone in a tiny cabin, where he did his own cooking in a none-too-clean kitchen. He also practiced his own kind of homegrown medicine. After Grandma's remark, everyone started recalling some old-time medical remedies. Aunt Mayme remembered that they once used rosemary and basil for an upset stomach. Aunt Clara said they were both good for vertigo. Mom recalled treating stomach complaints with something called dog fennel, Jerusalem oak, and marjoram.

"Wine," Grandma said. "Elderberry wine is good for an upset stomach."

No one questioned that.

Before that evening ended, the Lynks must have discussed a hundred different ailments, each with its own particular remedy. For extreme nervousness, there was lavender tea; for neuralgia, peppermint tea and horseradish poultices; rheumatism was relieved with a tea made of burdock leaves; arthritis was similarly treated, with goldenrod sometimes substituted for burdock; heart palpitations could be regulated with a tea made by brewing the bark of the black haw tree; diarrhea yielded to marjoram and, when available, calomel or opium; children's colic was sometimes treated with sarsaparilla or a tea made of cherry bark; goiter with fox glove; and the flu was sometimes treated with poultices made from flax seed and onions, followed by doses of sulphur and molasses.

Grandma Lynk.

Grandma Lynk closed the session with the dry remark that, when all else failed, a good shot of whiskey would usually take care of most any malady. Grandma Lynk was a caution. She would sit in her rocker, pleased to have her children and grandchildren near her, filling those around her with a feeling of love and acceptance, and—often without so much as saying a single word—giving us confidence and courage to face the world with dignity and a sense of pride and honor. A repository of family lore and history, Grandma Lynk was the one I should have asked about that side of my family, but Dad and I were on the train and halfway home the next day before I realized that I had failed to ask her one single question about the Lynks and her Burgrafs. By the way, a week later, as I was washing my hands, I looked down and the wart was gone!

As our summer vacation wound down, we boys from midtown turned to a game which we called "Shinny On Your Own Side." This game, like most of our games, was played in one form or another all up and down the valley, but the midtown version took on that special name when Walter's brother Bill warned Richard that if he didn't shinny on his own side, he might wish he had. In this game, you were in constant danger of either being clubbed to death or wounded by a flying piece of compacted tin. In order to play shinny you needed a tin can and several players, each equipped with a shillelagh-like stick, preferably one with a crooked or knobby end. The game was played sort of like ice hockey. There was a face-off at center court, followed by frantic beating and thrashing at the can, the object being to knock it across the opponent's goal line. When an opponent happened to step across an imaginary line from his side to your side, you had the right—yea, the duty!—to club him on his shins. These games grew progressively more intense as the can became compressed into an ever-smaller and potentially more lethal mass of metal. Although we midtown boys played this game in public view where everyone could see us, few of the boys from other neighborhoods ever asked to join in our games of shinny.

All of us Van Lear kids had chores to perform. I think it was a natural kind of thing that came from the work ethic that the Company expected from our fathers. My chores consisted of cutting kindling, gathering eggs, and hoeing in the garden. I hated hoeing in the garden. During this particular summer, Dad had me help him with our little garden plot in back of our house, and another spot near the Number One mine where we planted corn. Hoeing on that rocky hillside was really hard work. In our main garden, in addition to corn, lettuce, radishes, beans, cabbage, carrots, and tomatoes, we also grew potatoes, which sometimes attracted potato bugs when the plants were young and tender. One day, Dad had me go to the store to get some arsenic of lead to put on the potato plants, only when I got there I told Arlo that I wanted some arsenic and lace, and he told everybody within earshot and they all had a good laugh on me about that one.

Richard and I had just finished beating Walter and Billy in a game of shinny. We realized that we had better make the most of our freedom, for school would soon start up again. It was a Saturday in August, and we wanted to see the latest Tarzan movie but, as was often the case, we lacked the necessary cash. Richard's dad told us that we could clean out the mule barn, and for these services he would pay each of us a quarter, enough for a soda, a candy bar, and movie tickets, with a nickel to spare. The movie was a good one with Buster Crabbe as Tarzan, swinging from vines with the greatest of ease, yelling that great Tarzan yell of his before taking off on the back of a big elephant to mete out jungle justice to the bad men. When we emerged from the darkened hall that evening, our plans for the next few days had been decided by what we had just seen. We would build a tree house just like the Apeman's, complete with swinging grapevines. The only things we lacked were monkeys and elephants and natives, but with a little imagination we could even conjure them up.

For the tree house there was a wide variety of possible sites. Two favorite places were the Big Rocks, and John's Creek Hill, which some called Richmond Hill. The view from the Big Rocks, overlooking most of Miller's Creek, was one of the best, but for some reason we usually reserved that spot for spring and fall campouts. When Richard said he knew of a place with big wild grape vines not far above his house, that settled it. Once we had gotten our axes and other paraphernalia together, we met briefly at my house where my mother asked what we were intending to do, and after a convincing argument on my part, we set out. When we found the big vines Richard had told us about, we started hacking away at the underbrush, clearing a spot at the

The main mule barn where Richard and I earned movie money by cleaning out stalls for his father. When the barn was torn down, we scraped the concrete surface clean, put up a makeshift backboard, and played basketball on the old barn floor.

base of a huge oak, which had the makings of a perfect Tarzan Tree.

Although we were probably unaware of it or else wouldn't openly admit it, we young boys were attracted to the hills because of their great natural beauty as much as for any other single thing. The freedom to run and romp and play and act like Tarzan of the Apes was a part of it too, but there was more to it than that. The hills wove their own kind of magical spell over us.

"Look at this!" Bobby shouted. He had found some red, star-shaped plants. There were hundreds of them growing on the crest

Our beloved "Rec" building c. 1922, with a "Safety Meet" in progress. The second-floor theater served as the presentation hall for the town orchestra, visiting bands, and other entertainment. It was there that Richard and I and our buddies saw every cowboy movie ever made in the 1930s and early 1940s. This building burned shortly after it was acquired by Alf Duty and Herman Pack in the 1950s.

of the ridge. No one could identify the plants. In our wanderings we often found plants we knew something about like ginseng and mayapple, and lots of wild plants, flowers, and trees that seemed strangely out of place. Miss Harris had told us that this displaced northern flora was pushed to the south during the Glacial Age when many plants were forced by advancing ice and water onto the hills and valleys of southern Appalachia, where they had flourished and multiplied. I thought about this as we stood there admiring the view from the top of the hill, where we could look out over miles of Appalachian terrain, even into adjoining counties.

When we sat down to rest, Richard brought out his Boy Scout canteen filled with orange Nehi, and we took turns drinking from it.

"Hey, you guys," Billy yelled. He and Bobby were now further up the slope, exploring a crack in the earth. "Whadaya' think this is?" Billy asked, and we went over to him and got down on our knees and looked into a black and apparently bottomless split in the hilltop.

"It's a break in the earth," I told him.

"We know that, Spud," Billy said, "but why is it here? What made it?"

"It's from an earthquake maybe," I ventured, but I wasn't really sure. "It's from a long time ago," I added, but Richard and Bobby had some different ideas and, as was often the case, they were probably right.

"It's from the mine," Richard said.

"Sure," Bobby said, agreeing with Richard. "That's what it is." And then I remembered my dad saying something like that, and I didn't argue with them.

"There are slits like this all through the hills," Richard said. "When the miners pull the pillars of coal, the whole mountaintop drops. The whole thing splits and falls, and makes these slits in different places."

"Well," I said, hoping that I could show that I knew at least a little something about these kinds of things, "you're probably right, but they're just like what happens when there's an earthquake."

"I suppose so," Bobby reluctantly agreed, "only they call those kinds of slits 'faults' when they're caused by an earthquake."

While we were debating all of this, Billy began yelling down into the black cavernous chasm. "Hello," he said, and we could hear his voice echo back, and then Richard and I joined him, and pretty soon we were all yelling down into the split, and listening to the echoes reverberate off the walls and back. "Hell-oo... hell-oo ... hell-oo." It was an awesome experience, almost unreal.

When we tired of yelling into that hole in the ground, we went back down to the big oak tree, and turned to the task before us, but our attempt to build a tree house was short-circuited when Billy jumped out from behind a bush, yelling like a banshee. "There's a nest of copperheads here!" he shouted, running and waving his axe like a madman.

Billy's discovery moved all of us a bit farther down the slope where Richard located a flat place that was partially open, and it was here that we decided that we would build a cabin, not a tree-house. We were quite flexible back then, easily shifting into whatever the occasion required. A quick inspection found no snakes, and so we began our new enterprise by scraping off a place to position rocks for the foundation and the first round of logs.

That summer's cabin was a smaller version of our idea of the frontier cabins our pioneer ancestors built. There were numerous examples of these cabins still standing throughout our part of Kentucky. We had heard stories about such characters as Tice Harmon and Jenny Wiley, and other early settlers who once lived nearby in cabins not unlike the one we hoped to build.

Our cabin-building project went forward at a furious pace for the first week. Trees had to be felled and notched and placed in position, one on the other. Our families rarely saw us, except each morning when we left home and late in the evening when we returned too tired to do more than gather the eggs and kindling and then go to bed. We entered the second week with both energy and enthusiasm somewhat diminished, but the cabin was beginning to take shape, and the anticipation of its final completion spurred us on. Only a young Appalachian boy who has experienced the thrill of assembling a cabin on his own, unsupervised by interfering adults, aided only by his buddies and his trusty axe, can share the rapture of our experience. We interrupted work on the cabin only to attend to essential family chores like cutting firewood, hoeing in the garden, or, in the case of Richard, rounding up and milking his family's cows. So long as we did these chores, our parents seemed glad to have us involved in this kind of activity.

Ten days after we started the cabin, we placed the last bundle of sage grass onto the rafters to complete the roof. These shocks of dried grass were tied with seagrass rope, and then fastened to the poles which we used for rafters. We chinked the space between the logs with mud, and when that job was finished, Billy and Bobby went home to get gunny sacks for the bunks. When they returned Richard and I slit the ends of the brown bags and slipped them over pairs of poles, making stretcher-like cots for beds. After positioning these, one above the other on either side of the cabin, we then went outside to admire our handiwork. "This is our best one ever," Richard announced proudly.

"It's a good one all right," I agreed. Actually, it was the only cabin we had ever finished, roof and all.

Because we had planned to spend the night in the cabin, we had come fully prepared with food and cooking utensils, and so we set about the task of cooking our first meal. After performing a previously rehearsed dedicatory ritual, a combination cowboy and Indian sort of thing that we conjured up from a movie we had recently seen, we cooked and began to eat our supper. We had just started to eat when Billy ripped off an oath. "Damn," he cursed, "what's this?" He was holding aloft a long, brown thing he had fished from his plate. Our meal consisted of bacon and eggs mingled with dried leaves and twigs that had been blown into the skillets by gusty winds, topped off with baked potatoes and wood ashes, something we wouldn't touch if our moms had cooked it for us at home.

"That's a wood twig, Billy," I told him. "Eat it. It won't kill you." We said things like this to one another back then, imitating the tough men we saw in the movies.

Billy had brought sodas from the soda fountain where he worked part-time, and after we finished eating, Walter broke out the new cigarette machine that he had confiscated from his older brother, and commenced rolling tailor-mades, using what was left in his brother's tins of Bugle, and Prince Albert tobacco. None of us smoked cigarettes, but most of us had older brothers who did, and we had seen people like Jimmy Cagney and the like, and they were always smoking in the movies, and so we were determined to give it a try. When we used up all of the tobacco, Billy suggested that cornsilk and jimson weed made good smoking, but Bobby warned us about the poisonous properties of that combination, and suggested we try the dried leaves of some spike-headed plants that he had found growing in back of the community building. He had thoughtfully brought along some of these, so Walter rolled a few of them in his brother's machine. We sat on the flat rock ledge, and each of us lit one up. We were just beginning to enjoy the heady aroma, basking in a warm afterglow, when we suddenly heard a noise off in the gathering darkness. It could be anything! Bears, wolves, coyotes, and even panthers had been seen in these parts. Only Bobby had a gun, but it was a pea-shooter of a .22 and, worse still, it was all the way in back of the cabin on his bunk. So we just sat there, quiet as mice, waiting. Gradually it dawned on us. The crunching sounds were human footsteps on dried leaves. Someone was lurking out there near the cabin. That someone could see our little group by the campfire, but we couldn't see him, or them. "Don't move," Bobby counseled, "and don't say anything." None of us moved or said a word. Even though the glow from the firelight was dim, I could tell that Billy had turned pale and, as for myself, I don't mind admitting that I was really scared.

The waiting was worse than death. Finally, Richard broke the silence. "Come on in," he managed to blurt out. "You're welcome to join us." That sounded kind of silly, I thought, but none of us could think of anything else to say or do.

"Eee-yow-eee!" A bloodcurdling scream issued forth from the woods, now quite dark, and another in an even higher register. "Booo-ooo!" Then these cries were repeated as two figures came hurtling from the edge of darkness, both swathed in white.

Richard and I trailed Billy and Bobby by some thirty yards when we reached a flat spot above the Sparks barn, where we sat down on a rock to catch our breath. Except for our heavy breathing, everyone was strangely silent. After we rested a spell, we began to speculate about who it was and were they dangerous or just pranksters.

"There are some really bad people around here," Bobby said. "It could've been anyone." All of us agreed with that, and it occurred to me that they might have been some of those dangerous strangers my mom was always warning me about.

Finally, after we discussed the matter at some length, Billy, Walter, and Bobby decided to go on home, making excuses about chores they had to do. After they left, Richard and I just sat there for a while, not wanting to leave like the others. At last, screwing up courage, we decided to go back and defend our right to the cabin, or at least that's what we told each other we should do. But what motivated me, and I suspect Richard, was curiosity, wanting to know who it was that invaded our camp. And so we quietly began to retrace our steps.

When we arrived back at the plateau, the campfire was still burning, but there was no one in sight. We gathered up our utensils and slunk back home, but the next day we decided to concoct a story about what might have happened, and we started a newspaper, which we called *The Van Lear Gazette*. The first issue was immodestly devoted mostly to the cabin episode, partly true, and mostly fiction. The way we got out *The Gazette* was like this: Richard and I typed our stories on toy typewriters that our folks had bought for us. There were four pages in all, and it was necessary to retype each page since we didn't have any carbon paper, and no means of setting type or printing. The masthead was a homemade affair consisting of letters cut from rubber inner tubes which we glued onto a wooden block. We inked this and daubed it atop each of the first pages, and after several hours work, we proudly stood back to survey seven completed copies.

"Local Boys Save Cabin from Hoodlums!" our headline screamed. Our main story involved two fictitious toughies, who had tried to scare us off and take over our cabin. We filled the other three pages of our paper with local gossip and recipes that our mothers gave us. We sold only three or four copies of that first edition, and no one seemed to believe our story, or even pay much attention to it.

When Walter and his older brother Bill saw our little creation, they went home and started up their own competing newspaper, which they called *The Van Lear Dispatch*, and for the next two weeks we got out these tabloids, and sold them for a nickel a copy. When we ran out of news, we ceased publication of both papers, and no one seemed to miss them, least of all our moms, who had grown tired of telling us gossipy things we could write up.

We never did learn who had tried to scare us that night at our cabin site, but we did return to the cabin one more time. Unfortunately, one of us lit a match too close to an overhead bunk, setting fire to the flammable gunny sack, which quickly spread to the grass-thatched roof. We spent that night sleeping on the ground, outside the now-gutted cabin.

We searched for ways to entertain ourselves and our friends as that summer vacation rapidly drew to a close. For the better part of the next week, Richard and I and Billy and Bobby, curtained off a section under Richard's front porch and presented a play that Richard and I had written or, I should say, a play we imagineered, since we really hadn't written anything down on paper. The version we finally presented was much amended, reflecting the demands of Billy and Bobby as their price for agreeing to take part in it. The original story line revolved around three main characters like The Three Musketeers, but after the audience's intervention, the play more nearly resembled a Three Stooges cartoon, with the fourth character, played by Billy, acting more like Amos and Andy, although he was supposed to be D'Artagnan. Once we were satisfied with it, we declared our most recent rehearsal as final, and we invited Richard's sister Darlene and asked her to tell Ann and Peggy Beers and Doris Ann Harris that they could come too. Most of our buddies declined our invitation, but Walter and Bill showed up, so we had a pretty good audience, and the six of them and we four performers pretty much filled up all of the open space under the Sparks's front porch.

Richard made the introduction, it being his house and all, and he then went back behind the burlap curtain, and we began the opening scene, which had me and Bobby all decked out in bathrobes, with Bobby also wearing a plumed hat that belonged to his mother. Both of us had wooden swords stuck in the sashes of our robes. We were two of the three musketeers, and we were waiting for the third one, and since that was Richard, we had to wait around and improvise while he finished putting on his costume, and so we did this by making up idle conversation.

"Alas, Aphos," Bobby said, "we must await the arrival of our companion, Aristes. Have you heard any word of his whereabouts, perchance?"

"No, Portsmouth," I replied, "I perchance have not. We canst but wait some more."

As you can see, our memory of the actual names of the principal characters was faulty, and we could hear titters from our audience. Darlene spoke up and said, "It's Athos, Porthos, and Aramis, dummies!" And, when she said this, everyone laughed except Bobby and me.

"And where's D'Artagnan?" Doris yelled out, encouraged by Darlene, and this really caused a riot of laughter.

Then Peggy put another nail in our coffin by telling us that there was a fifth character, a guy named Richelieu who was the queen's nemesis. "He was a cardinal or something like that," she said.

Then Richard turned the whole thing upside down when he came out in his costume, which was one of his mother's old corsets tied with a rope around his waist. He had a fake mustache and someone's Masonic high top hat and a sword, and he was supposed to be Aramis, but he had changed his name to Aristes. As soon as he showed up from behind the curtain, the girls roared, and old Aristes had to wait for what seemed like a minute or more before he could speak. By then I guess Bobby decided that the only sensible thing to do was to change the whole thing into a full-fledged comedy, and so he strutted out in front of Richard and me, and announced that he had found Cardinal Richelieu and had taken him captive. "Methinks," Portsmouth-Bobby said with a great flourish, "the cardinal was setting a trap for her majesty, the queen."

"Then," Aristes-Richard said, "bring him to us at once."

"Yes," I added in my best Aphos voice, "by all means, Aristes, bring the rascal here, that we may deal with this dastardly person."

Bobby went back through the curtain and then returned, this time with Billy-D'Artagnan in tow, holding him by his right ear. Billy was wearing one of his mother's aprons with a dagger stuck down inside it. "Here," Portsmouth-Bobby said, as he pushed Billy down onto the dirt floor. "Here is the filthy culprit, Cardinal Richelieu."

Billy thought he was supposed to be D'Artagnan, the friend of the three musketeers, and so he lay there for a few moments and then he got up, dusted himself off, and in his high-pitched nasal voice said, "Hey, brother Kingfish, I thought you was bringing me to the lodge hall. What's this Cardinal Rich-lou business, anyway?"

From there, it became even more ridiculous, but our audience seemed to enjoy the rest of our little show. To us it didn't seem so strange, as we had witnessed adult plays and movies we thought almost as silly

And so the curtain descended on another summer in our town of Van Lear, a summer filled with memories of hard-fought baseball games, family visits, and cabins built on the steep hillsides above town, but, most of all, a summer of deepening bonds with my buddies. The coming fall would provide even more golden memories.

Chapter Three
Miss Hobson's Fourth Grade

He who seeks no knowledge of his forebears
dishonors both himself and his ancestors.
                                    —Anonymous

The summer of 1934 has ended and, alas, school has begun. To most of us children, "school" is regarded as another season, one that stretches all the way through fall and winter, and into much of

The Central Grade School building at Van Lear, where excellent teachers held forth, stretching our youthful minds and imaginations with assignments like Miss Hobson's family-theme project.

spring, a sad, but necessary interruption to our boyhood pursuits. Reluctantly, we leave the hills and our summertime games and return to the classroom at Van Lear Central Graded School.

Custodian Jim King.

As Marcus and Richard and Worth and I enter the gray, two-story building, the smell of freshly oiled wood floors greets us at the front door. Custodian Jim King has the place ready for us, teacher and pupil alike. Soon the slightly acrid aroma of pencil shavings will fill the air, an odor that haunts me to this very day. We wait until the last minute to find our way to Miss Doris Hobson's fourth grade classroom. There it is, across the hall from Miss Bessie's third grade, right behind Miss Adams' second grade, catty-cornered and down the hall from Miss Suzy Risner's first grade. We look longingly up the wide front staircase. Next year, we will be in Miss Anderson's room, members of the elite fifth grade. Until then, only those who are a year or two older than us are privileged to know the mysteries of that noble and exalted realm. We join Betty and Ilene and her cousin Billie Jean, and Ann and Maxine, Arnold, Ralph, and Charles, and a dozen other pupils. Miss Hobson greets us, quickly assigns our seats, and in no time at all, we have been told to get out our history books.

"Who knows what these three men had in common?" Miss Hobson gets right to the point. We wait to hear their names. "Coronado, Cortez, and

Our fourth-grade teacher Doris Hobson.

DeSoto." She pronounces their names slowly and deliberately, and awaits our response.

Finally, Marcus speaks up. "They're all Spanish," he says, and Miss Hobson says that's right and what else, and I raise my hand, and Miss Hobson nods in my direction.

"All three of them were explorers," I venture a guess, having recalled something to that effect from some prior learning.

"That's correct," she says, adding, "and now open your history books and we'll read about two of these men, and some English explorers as well. We'll also learn more about the men and women who were early pioneers right here in eastern Kentucky." We open our books and begin reading. It never occurs to us to do otherwise. This is 1934, and our parents support the teachers absolutely, completely, and without question. And despite our reluctance to reenter the classroom and leave our summer fun behind, our teachers have a way of making this sort of thing entertaining.

As we read, we learn that the effects of early Spanish exploration and settlement in this country are most evident along the Florida and California coasts, places only vaguely familiar to us land-locked Appalachian kids, yet our imaginations run rampant with visions of those faraway lands. We learn that DeSoto, Cortez, and Coronado led expeditions throughout the South and Southwest, some of them even into Mexico during the 16th century. Our book's authors tell us that they found few riches, and left fewer permanent settlements, except at Saint Augustine in Florida, and later at a few Spanish missions in California. It seems that there is little evidence of Spanish culture in the North American interior. We can relate to that. None of us has ever seen anything remotely resembling anything Spanish in these parts.

Taking turns, we continue to read, this time about the first efforts to establish a permanent English colony in North America. Richard raises his hand and, after getting permission to speak, asks, "Miss Hobson, whatever happened to Cortez?"

I should explain that my classmate Richard is Richard Adams, not my other friend with the same first name, Richard Sparks. Miss Hobson fields his question neatly. She is unfailingly fair and considerate. "We'll learn more about him later, Richard," she says. "Hernando Cortez spent a great deal of time in Cuba and Mexico, and in Southern California. He is generally credited with the discovery of the Gulf of California. Today, and for the next several days, we shall study those persons—mostly Spanish and English —whose early explorations led to the settlement of our part of the New World."

Richard nods, and we continue. It is now Ann's turn to read. Sir Walter Raleigh, we are told, financed the first English colony in this country in 1584. Disease and death decimated the first group. In 1591, a second colony of one hundred men, women, and children replaced them, but they disappeared without a trace. Miss Hobson sends Richard to the map on the wall, and tells him to find the place where Raleigh's colony was located. After he does this, Miss Hobson nods her approval, and he returns to his seat.

We discuss Raleigh at some length. We learn that it was he who introduced the western world to the redman's curse, tobacco. We learn some new words such as "chivalrous act," "courtly manner," and "gentlemanliness," but, for the life of us, we cannot fathom why a man would lay down his good coat over a mudhole, even for a queen! We are pleased to learn that, while the early Spanish explorers often treated the native inhabitants of the Americas with contempt, the English colonists were, for the most part, more compassionate in their dealings with the people Columbus called Indians. With rare exceptions, our history book tells us, the English settlers tried to make friends with the natives, often seeing it as their duty to instill in them their own culture, their own brand of Christianity, and their own ideas of what constituted civilization. We don't always agree with this. Our sympathies are usually with the Indians. Strange, isn't it, how children sense the rightness of most things, almost without thinking.

We break for recess after Miss Hobson promises us that we will resume our reading and discussion when we return. Can you imagine this? We can't wait to return to those stories in our history books! But then, there is no television in 1934. Not only is there no televi-

Tom Ghee and Harvey Michaels. We visited the Michaels house on Slate Row to hear the election returns late one November night in 1932. I wasn't wearing the Hoover button that I had worn in 1928, and Franklin D. Roosevelt won.

sion, for many there is still no radio. My family now owns a radio, but I recall walking a mile or so with my parents to the Harvey Michael's house on Slate Row just two years ago to listen to news of the Roosevelt-Hoover presidential election returns. Those of us whose families have radios tell the others about everything they're missing, and they listen enviously to the stories of daring-do from the likes of Jack Armstrong, and the comic antics of Ed Wynn and Joe Penner.

A five-minute recess doesn't allow much time for hill climbing, so we amuse ourselves in the schoolyard, jumping ditches, climbing trees, playing marbles, or watching the older boys wrestle.

Miss Hobson welcomes us back to our classroom with a question. "What kinds of people settled America?" she asks.

Our answers are varied. Betty says mostly farmers, Arnold says they were good, law-abiding folks. Ann seems to win the prize for the best answer when she responds, "All kinds of people, Miss Hobson, but mostly God-fearing people in search of religious freedom."

We continue our reading. We learn that one little-known aspect of early colonization was the apprenticeship of orphans. Miss Hobson asks us if we know the meanings of some of these words. When no one responds, she puts aside our history textbook, and reaches for another. "This," she announces, pointing to a black-covered, official-looking book, "is a copy of *Abstract Proceedings of the Virginia Company of London of 1619-1624.*"

Never mind that word, "abstract," nor the adult content of the book Miss Hobson now holds opened in her hand. Our teachers pull no punches. They use few euphemisms, and make fewer efforts to spare us the pain of learning words beyond our immediate ken. These practices are a part of the legacy left by early school superintendents Forest Bell and Carlos V. Snapp, men who carried out the mandate of their employers, mine superintendents like Jack Price, whose own nephew attended our schools. Reared back east in the more refined atmosphere of his juvenile upbringing, Price had brought with him teachers like his sister-in-law, Margaret Motter, who had matriculated at Hood College in Frederick, Maryland, and Kitty Bess Dobson and others, all of whom set a high mark for local scholars and future teachers. Those of us who sat that day in Miss Hobson's fourth grade class were beneficiaries of that lasting legacy. The dictum that one must stretch one's mind if one is to learn, first begun under Bell and Snapp, was now being continued throughout the Van Lear schools under the supervision of people like John Squire Reed, Verne P. Horne, and Jesse Holland, the high school's football coach.

I thought once to complain to my mother and father about how difficult school was, but I did this only once, which was more than enough. It seems that, although they only completed the eighth grade in a one-room school, their learning regimen was even more difficult and demanding than ours. My ill-advised complaint had been directed to my father as he sat on our porch one evening, reading his newspaper. It went something like this: "I wish school was easier," I said.

This caused Dad to lay his paper aside, remove his reading glasses, and commence to lecture me. "You don't know what you're talking about, young man," he said. "School was much more difficult when your mother and I were your age."

As Dad outlined all that they had been taught, I soon realized that their eighth-grade education had been even more difficult than my brother and sister's high schooling.

"Did you have to write a family history?" I asked.

"Not only that, son," Dad said, "but we had to do a lot of other things."

I felt like saying "like what?" but I didn't and I didn't have to, as Dad told me about their curriculum without any prompting on my part.

"We had to name nine rules for using capital letters and give examples, we had to define the parts of speech and name those that had no modifiers, we had to name the principal parts of a verb and give examples, we had to know the rules of punctuation, and we had to write a theme on all the epochs into which U.S. History is divided."

"Will we learn all that?" I asked.

"I hope so, son," he said, and then he continued. "You should also learn the names and locations of all the mountains in this country, all the rivers, and all of our trade centers, and maybe even things like orthography."

"What's that?"

"Rules for our written language, things like language sounds, spelling rules, prefixes, suffixes, and word roots. All that."

"Listen to this," Miss Hobson says, interrupting my thoughts. "Try to imagine yourself an orphaned child in London, three hundred years ago," our teacher says, and with that she begins to read from the hard-bound book she is holding. "There shall be dispatched from London to Virginia one hundred children, all orphans, for apprenticeship periods which shall endure at the least seven years, if they live so long. They shall be educated, cared for, taught a trade or profession, and shall be given fifty acres to hold in fee simple by socage tenure to every of them and their heirs, freely at the rent of 12d. by the year, in full of all rents or other payment of service due unto the Lord, therefore to be rendered or done." Miss Hobson closes the book, places it back on her desk, and asks us what we think about that bit of history.

Several of us have opinions. Worth thinks that this was a pretty good thing for children who were orphans. Richard agrees. Ilene wonders how well they were treated. Billie Jean says it was probably better than being put in an orphanage. Maxine thinks so too. I'm not so sure. After all, how do we know what it was like back then, either in an orphanage or as an apprenticed orphan in America? Richard wonders if any of our ancestors were apprenticed orphans. Miss Hobson suggests that we should ask our parents about our families, and in class we would each make a family tree, and write an essay about our ancestors. That will be a project she will expect from each of us before the first semester of school ends. We now hear about the family history project for which Miss Hobson is so widely known.

We take our lunches to school. At noon, we retrieve our brown bags or lunch pails from the cloakroom, and then we go outside and find a place under a beechnut tree, not far up the hillside from the school building. It is still warm, unseasonably warm for September. Our ritual is soon established during the first week of school. If Richard has bologna and I have peanut butter, then we swap, half a bologna for half a peanut butter. Egg salad sandwiches are best, but sloppy. And homemade biscuits or cornbread are not so good. We think that machine-sliced light bread is better than home-baked bread. For most of us, an apple is our dessert. After eating lunch, we return for an afternoon of arithmetic and spelling drill and practice.

On the way home, we pause briefly near the brick powder magazine behind the big store. No one in our group can remember when this little fortress-like structure was used to store blasting material. Marcus recalls his dad telling him that this particular one was used when old Mine No. 152 was operating. Richard begins to laugh, and he tells us a story that had been told to his dad about one young miner who decided if he had two daughters and a son, he would name them Monybell, Jellybell, and Dynamite, names of three types of blasting material used in the mines.

We loiter a while longer. We are in no particular hurry to go on home, although someone may ask us what took us so long when we do get there. Most of the adults are good to us. They leave us alone, and we try our best to avoid them. It's a good arrangement for both sides. Except for varsity school sports, and church and school-sponsored plays and things like that, few adults try to organize us or supervise us in any of our activities. We like it this way. Richard has found a big cardboard box, back of the main store, and we bend it into a long, flat piece, and use it to slide down the slick brown sage grass on the slope next to the powder magazine.

Some of the big boys are trotting down to the football field where they will practice. The field is more than a mile away, and Coach Jesse Holland has his boys run all the way down and back. It's good for them, he says. We step aside as Malcolm Shearer, Howard Sparks, and Dick Stapleton trot by. Maybe we'll go watch them practice. Later, we could go over to the Garland Webb farm and watch the Webbs make sorghum. But then I remember I have to cut kindling wood, and Richard and Marcus have chores to do, so we hurry home.

Suppertime was always a big event with most Van Lear families. Miners' families usually ate well. Ours was no exception. One reason the miner chose to be a miner was to earn more money than other wage earners, considerably more than hillside farmers, and thus be able to provide more for their families. And most families raised a garden. Ours did, and Mom always canned lots of stuff like green beans, tomatoes, corn, blackberries, jelly, and lots of pickled cabbage and kraut. Although the entire country was now caught up in an economic depression, most of us never knew it. Our parents sometimes spoke of it, and we would see headlines alluding to it, or if a family had a radio they would hear Lowell Thomas speak of it, but mostly we were blissfully ignorant of anything so arcane, unless our dads were laid off when the output of the mines couldn't be sold by the Company, something that had begun to happen more often lately.

On this night, after supper, I sit with Dad and Mom on the porch of our little company house, and try to turn the subject of our conversation to family and early ancestors, hoping to get a head start on Miss Hobson's semester theme assignment. Finally, Dad puts down his newspaper to listen to my nagging questions.

"Why do you want to know so many things about family?" Dad asks.

"Because," I say, hoping that will suffice.

"Because why?" he persists.

"Because I have to write a theme this semester about family," I say.

With that brief explanation, Dad relents, and tries to help, perhaps recalling his earlier lecture to me about how much more difficult his school days had been. "Well," he says, "on our side, you know that your grandfather is my father, Anthony Wayne Vaughan, and his wife, your grandmother, is America McBrayer Vaughan. She grew up in Carter County, Kentucky, Pap in Wayne County, Virginia, which is now West Virginia. Pap's dad was James Vaughan. I was named for him. He grew up on a farm owned by his dad Thomas, near the mouth of the Big Sandy. That's about it, son. For your mother's side, you'll have to ask her."

I can tell that Dad is hoping that this will suffice. He picks up his paper again. "Who was Thomas Vaughan's father?" I ask, hoping Dad has more information on his side of our family.

"William Vaughan was his name," Dad says, "but I'm afraid I don't know too much more about that."

"Is that who Granddad and Cousin Willie were talking about last summer?" I ask, recalling the visit of Willie Vaughan, a previously undiscovered cousin from Tampa, Florida, who happened in on us a year ago at a time when Granddad Vaughan was also visiting us.

"That's right, son," Dad says, adding nothing more to family lore.

"Tell him what you know, Jim," Mom says, trying to be helpful.

"Well?" I ask.

"Well, what?" Dad says and I can tell he really isn't planning to be all that talkative about family. His "Pap," my granddad, is the talkative one, the one who spins tall tales, and sometimes dredges up facts and information that would otherwise be lost.

"Well, what about the story about Vaughans from Wales?" I ask. "What about the place Granddad said we came from, Tretower, I think he called it?"

"I don't know about that for a fact, son," Dad says. "Better ask Pap next time we see him. He knows more about that. He'll visit again sometime this year."

Mom had already gone into the house to do her evening chores, so I would corner her some other time and see if I could get some information out of her about the Lynks and Burgrafs. At least I know that her mother's people, the Burgrafs, came from Holland.

The Sparks family kept horses and cows, and Richard had inherited his brother Howard's role as cowboy and farmhand. As a reward for his work, Richard had a spotted pony, and sometimes the two of us would ride the little Shetland around the hillside, down and in back of the football field, where we would round up their cows and herd them back home for milking. Richard's dad still used horses to deliver coal and groceries. One day we learned that one of the larger animals had dropped dead near the football field, and Mister Sparks wanted to perform an autopsy to see what ended its life. Richard and I rode his pony around the hillside early that evening, and squatted down behind the huge, bloated roan horse, and watched the operation. Garland Webb and Shade Ward had joined Mister Sparks, and it was Shade who made the incision.

My friend Richard Sparks on his pony, which we often rode "double" around the hillside to the football field to collect his family's cows.

"Whoosh!" A loud rush of air came forth from the animal's bulging belly, followed by the most noxious odor we had ever smelled.

Both of us jumped backwards, and then, holding our noses, we ventured forward to peer inside the carcass, where a purple liver now lay exposed. "Cholera?" one of the men speculated, but the general consensus was that the horse had eaten something that had poisoned him.

If baseball was the king of sports in Van Lear, football was its prince, and basketball only a distant duke. One fine morning around the first of September, Van Lear boys would awaken fully aware in their subconscious minds that it was time to play football. No one announced this, although the cooler breezes that moderated the stifling heat may have heralded it, and the sight of the varsity boys trotting down to the football field in their practice uniforms had a lot to do with the changing of the sports seasons. But mostly, though, it was just a feeling all up and down Miller's Creek as boy-thoughts turned away from lesser pursuits to concentrate on the sport of Knute Rockne, George "The Gipper" Gipp, and Red Grange.

Our early fall routine was similar to the one we followed during spring baseball season. There were no little leagues or prep or grade school organizations for any sport. No adults helped or interfered. Every sport was kid sport, self-organized games played on the sandlot nearest each of the neighborhoods up and down the valley. Although the games were impromptu, there was a certain kind of formality to them. Each game was arranged about a week in advance when the word went out, for instance, that our Barnyard Gang in midtown wanted to play the boys from Possum and Sorghum Hollow. This would give each team a few days to recruit players and practice. There were usually five or six neighborhood teams ready to provide spirited competition. At West Van Lear, Perry McCloud, Worth Goble, and their group had a team. Then, at the River, Kenneth and Jack Preston, Jack Rogers, Boone, Charles, and Ernest Soards, and Clifford Honaker could usually round up a team. Marcus and Charles Spears, Billy and Earl Rucker, Richard Adams, and the Conleys, Fishers, and Pelphreys made up the Bradley Crossing team. In our part of town, Oakley Picklesimer and Spider Webb sometimes had their own team, and at other times joined our team. The boys from Sorghum Hollow, Possum Hollow, and Silk Stocking Row sometimes fielded a team, or else the Bowlings, Kretzers, and Youngs would join forces with Russell Rice and the Wills boys from Music Hollow and Slate Row. Rounding out the town's informal sandlot teams were the guys at Mine No. 5: John and Hondel Adams, Teamus Bowling, Leo Perkowski, Bill Ditty, Jimmy Campigotto, Frankie Cunningham, Tony Clifton, and, on occasion, the Butcher and Kretzer boys.

Of the Barnyard boys, only Bobby and Howard Russell had any real football equipment. Howard Russell had his older brother Harold's helmet, and Bobby had a pair of shoulder pads given him by his cousin Bill. Richard owned a real-leather football. When we learned that Howard Russell's brother Harold had won his leather helmet by selling three one-year subscriptions to the *Saturday Evening Post*, Richard and I found a magazine ad that described that premium. The ad was so seductive, we immediately sent off for the necessary forms, but failing to get the required six subscriptions, we played out the remainder of the sandlot football season without any headgear. Several of our gang had our mothers stitch navy blue numerals onto gray sweatshirts, and it was in this sort of regalia that the Barnyard Gang took the field. Much as we would have liked to have had a full season of games, two or three match-ups usually proved the limit of our endurance, whereupon we then started watching the big boys.

During the fall and winter months, we turned our attention to another form of entertainment. There was no television to numb the mind and soul. Instead there was radio, but radio didn't dull the senses like television. Radio was different back then, not the glorified jukebox it would later become. Radio didn't take over your life; instead, it opened up your mind. In fact, to us Van Lear boys, radio was theater of the mind, a vast, seamless, panoramic window on the world through which we could imagine all sorts of things. Dad bought our radio, a Crosley, at the Van Lear commissary for forty dollars soon after consoles replaced those old models that had separate speakers. It wasn't one of those cathedral-shaped things that sat on a table, but a real piece of furniture that stood upright on the floor, glowing out at you from its yellowish tuning dial as though it were alive. Richard's family had a fancier Zenith. Billy's family's radio was a Philco. Jack's family had the best one in town, a Sonora, the Neurodyne Model 242 with an "all-wood tone chamber." Jack said his folks bought it the year he was born, and it cost over two hundred dollars, an unimaginable sum. I remember what they paid for it because for a couple hundred more, you could have bought a new Ford automobile.

As a part of the fall football ritual Richard and I spent most Saturday evenings listening to college scores on the radio. The first scores came in from the small eastern schools like Lafayette and Lehigh, Susquehanna, Slippery Rock and Shippensburg; then the bigger ones: Fordham, Columbia, Yale, Harvard, Princeton, Dartmouth, Army; and still later the big midwestern and southern schools: Notre Dame and Michigan, Georgia Tech and Alabama; and then, finally, late at night there were the west coast schools: UCLA, USC, and Stanford. As we listened to the scores, we sometimes even drew pictures of players in big leather headgear, and then we painted the helmets in each school's colors: Harvard crimson and white, Yale blue, Pennsylvania red and blue, Princeton black and orange, Michigan blue and gold.

College football games were brought to life by the golden voices of radio's Bill Stern, and later by Red Barber and Mel Allen, sports announcers who broadcast just enough aural information to stimulate our fertile imaginations to heights that would be undreamed of in the soon-to-be too-graphic age of television. All of this was enhanced and glamorized and made even more vivid by collegiate music like the "Notre Dame Fight Song," "On Wisconsin," and everyone's favorite, "Hail To Thee, Cornell."

Bob Gunning, Bobby's dad, had more interesting hobbies than anyone else we knew in Van Lear. He made neat model airplanes

Bob Gunning is at the left and Clark Dillon at the right, c. 1922. The father of my good friend, Bobby, Mister Gunning was a master model-maker and ham radio operator who sometimes let us look in on his hobbies.

and ships, and had a ham radio rig, which was connected to a wire aerial strung all the way across the valley. On occasion, he would allow us to stand quietly nearby and listen as he CQ'd other ham operators around the world. You can imagine how this impressed impressionable young boys like us. And, on cool evenings when the wind was calm, Mister Gunning would sometimes bring out one of his model planes and, after using a hand drill to tightly twist the strands of rubber that powered the propeller, he would send the craft flying off in a wide arc, high above our heads, a scene Richard and I could never emulate when we tried to duplicate this feat with one of our own crudely constructed models.

During the winter months Richard and I sometimes got together and listened to radio while doing homework. We didn't do a lot of homework, but our parents thought we did. The programs we listened to were really neat. There were "Jack Armstrong, the All-American Boy," and "Terry and The Pirates," programs that transported us in our youthful imaginations on all sorts of adventures, stories that entertained us and held our attention. We supplied the drama in the form of our own mental images of what was happening. We listened to radio shows like "Ma Perkins," "Death Valley Days," "Lux Radio Theater," and "One Man's Family," with old Father Barber telling his "bewildering offspring" how things used to be back even earlier than the 1930s, all the while sighing and muttering in resignation to his long-suffering wife Fannie. Whenever she asked him something, you knew what old Father Barber's answer would be. It was always, "Yes, Fannie, yes," no matter what the question. Despite the old man's boredom or whatever, there was something about the way they treated one another that made you know they were good folks to be around, just like "Pepper Young's Family."

There were very few crime stories on the radio, and in the few dramas that did involve crime, the criminal always got his just desserts quickly, like on "Mr. District Attorney," who was billed as "Champion of the People" and "Defender of Truth."

Richard, Bobby, Buddy, Walter, and I sent off for a lot of the premiums offered on the radio programs, things like the decoder pins that you could get for a quarter and the foil inner lining from an Ovaltine container, as promised on "Little Orphan Annie." We knew that those radio people were doing all of this just to get us to drink Ovaltine, but there was also a special feeling about sending off for the stuff, and then visiting the post office in anticipation of its arrival, sort of like our parents used to experience when they got things delivered to them by the Wells Fargo Wagon.

Some of the sponsors, like the makers of Wheaties, offered Babe Ruth signet rings or baseballs with the Babe's autograph stamped on them, or hiking calculators, which were things you strapped onto your belt and they would count your steps and give you a digital readout of how far you walked. Richard and I each had one of those things, which we tore apart only to discover that they never worked right when we put them back together. But, when we learned about automatic watches, we understood the pendulum principle behind them, thanks to our experience tearing apart the hiking calculators.

During the cold winter months we were very loyal listeners, even to those shows that didn't offer any premiums. "Inner Sanctum" with its scary stories was a favorite. There was one "Inner Sanctum" episode in particular during Halloween that I remember. Richard and I were doing homework and only half-listening. First there was this creaky door. Then a voice. "Perhaps, young man," this weird voice said, "you would like to join me on my venture."

Well, what was that all about? We strained to hear more. This old guy with the ghoulish voice invited this young kid to go with him into this old house—you could tell it was old by the creaky old door and floors—and nobody lived there and it was all cold and spooky, with the wind howling and an owl hooting. My first thought was, why in God's name would that kid want to follow that old ghoul into that old house? Anyway, Richard and I set our books aside and started listening more closely. My folks had gone to a town meeting, and except for Old Lucky, who was lying there in front of the fireplace half asleep, we were all alone. It was deathly still, but we could hear the wind rustling the leaves, and, off in the distance, the lonesome whistle of a coal train, and there were those creaky floors and the owl and the wind, and it got to the point where we couldn't tell if it was real or on the radio.

The man and the boy were waiting for someone to meet them in the old house, when all of a sudden the old guy and the kid start hearing a sound like a leaky faucet, and then the boy lets out a yell when he feels something warm and moist dripping on him from the ceiling.

"What's this?" the boy asked, and you could tell he was scared when he said it. "What's this gooey stuff?"

"Where?" the old ghoul asked.

"Here on my face," the kid said, and you could tell he was getting really scared. "Something dripped on my face. Light a match, mister. What is this?"

The dripping sound stopped, and there was the sound of a match striking. "There," the man said, "now we shall see, my young friend."

The boy let out a scream. "What is it?" the man asked.

"Blood!" the boy said, and at that moment there was this dramatic and somber chord sounded by the studio organ.

"It's blood all right," the old man said, "and it's coming from the ceiling right over our heads."

The ominous organ chord sounded once more as Richard and I sat there, textbooks closed, mouths open, our hearts pounding in our ears.

"Who is it?" the boy asked. "Who's up there?"

"I don't know," the man said. And then, addressing his question to the ceiling, he asked, "Who are you?" which, to Richard and me, seemed a really dumb thing. Most people dripping blood from a ceiling would be dead, we reasoned.

A spooky banshee kind of sound moaned in time with the whirling wind outside our house, and the radio announcer came on to tell us that the story would continue in a moment, right after a word from the sponsor. The wind began to howl again, our old house began to creak, and then a voice from above seemed to be saying, "Raw head and bloody bones!" Richard and I could hear it, plain as day, but I had turned the volume down. Yet there it was again!

Just then, my dad burst in through the front door, screaming at the top of his lungs like a raving maniac, my mother in close pursuit. "Stop it, Jim," Mom said, "You'll scare them to death. Now, stop it!"

They almost had to scrape me and Richard off the ceiling, and both of us admitted to each other the next day that we had trouble getting to sleep that night, but that disclosure came only after we swore each other to secrecy. After all, our reputations as the brave young men who had conquered the cabin invaders might be at stake.

Granddad visited us right after Thanksgiving. After we put away Mom's turkey dinner, complete with the oyster dressing and fresh cranberry sauce that Dad loved so much, I started asking Granddad all sorts of questions about our family. He was glad to comply, as he loved to tell stories, especially about kinfolk; he could go on for hours, without repeating himself. My first question set him off. "Tell me about old William Vaughan," I urged.

Grandfather Anthony Wayne Vaughan, his wife America McBrayer Vaughan, (seated), and members of their family, c. 1914. My father, James, was not present for this photo. Among those pictured are, back row, left to right, Mattie Wolf Vaughan, her husband John (holding son Delbert), Everett Vaughan, Gladys Fultz, Ida Vaughan Ball, Wayne Vaughan, Ruben Ball, Will Vaughan, Toby Vaughan, and Howard Vaughan. Standing between Anthony Wayne and America is Lester Ball. Seated at the right is Norma Hall, daughter of Ella Vaughan and Noah Hall. It was Granddad Anthony Wayne who first told me about our Welsh Tretower Vaughans. Many years later Uncle Everett put me on the trail of "Old William" and his wife, Fereby Benton Vaughan. Miss Hobson's fourth-grade family theme project helped whet my appetite for family history, a practice I strongly recommend to revitalize an interest in history in present-day public and private schools.

"You mean my great granddad?" Granddad asked, knowing that was who I had in mind. "Well now," he said, "let's see. He would be your great-great-great granddad."

He then told me everything he could think of about Old William, as he called him, how he was said to have been a Welshman who traded with the Cherokee Indians, back in the 1700s, how he had married a part-Cherokee woman named Fereby Benton and then homesteaded land in the far western regions of Virginia, how he was drafted into Colonel Preston's brigade and served under a Captain David Looney, along with people like Daniel Boone, during Lord Dunmore's War. That's where I had to stop him. I knew something about Boone, but who was this Lord Dunmore.

"He was the last Colonial Governor of Virginia," Granddad said. "The reason he recruited a volunteer army was the Shawnee Indians had sent word that they were going to kill the white scouts who were exploring the far western reaches of Virginia, the part that is now the state of Kentucky. The Indians didn't like anyone to settle on that territory, which they regarded as their sacred buffalo hunting ground. Dunmore ordered Colonel Preston to send some of his men west to warn the scouts, and Preston passed the order on to Captain Looney, who sent Boone and another man to find the scouts. They found them at the falls of the Ohio River and returned with them to the east, probably saving their lives, but the war continued, off and on, for most of the year of 1774."

I never questioned how Granddad knew all of this because I also knew that he read a lot. In fact, he told me more than once, "Whatever you do in your life, always read. Read everything you can find. It will serve you well."

"And William Vaughan was in the same company as Daniel Boone?" I asked.

"That's right, James," he said. "It's right there in the old journals.

"What else can you tell me about him, Grandpa?" I asked.

"Well, I'm sorry to say, not all that much. His oldest son, Thomas, settled on land even farther to the west in Wayne County, Virginia. That's Cabell County in West Virginia now. Pap grew up there, but when he married my mother, Susannah Wilson, they moved across the Big Sandy to the Kentucky side, and that's where I was born. Thomas' mother and father, Fereby and old William, moved on into Tennessee, and settled somewhere in northwestern Arkansas. That's what our Cousin Willie and I were talking about last year when he visited."

Cousin Willie Vaughan and his dog Rascal, at home in Tampa, Florida, c. 1934. Family discussions by Cousin Willie and Grandpa Vaughan concerning our Welsh heritage are etched forever in my memory and played an important role in shaping my later life.

I sat there, listening intently.

"Like I said, Willie and I couldn't come up with anything more on old William, but both of us had heard stories, handed down in each of our families, about our Vaughans' place in southern Wales, a place called Tretower, which means place of the castle tower. Pap's dad told him, and he passed it on to me. The property at Tretower was given to Roger Vaughan in 1450 by William Herbert. It was owned by our Vaughans until 1783, when it was sold to a family named Parry. Granddad Thomas was born in 1773, and would have been ten years old at the time. His father, William, knew about the homeplace, and when he learned that it had been sold, he passed this information along to Thomas, who passed it on to my father, and he to me, and so on, and you should pass it on to keep it alive."

"Wow!" I said.

"Yes, my boy," granddad said, "that's something worth keeping alive, and there's even more I can tell you, but I'm afraid not much more about old William."

"Oh?"

"We lost track of that branch of the family. And we never learned who our original immigrant Welsh ancestor was, but I don't believe it was William. I believe he was also part Indian, just like his wife. I did read a lot, and learned a lot more about other things, and you should too. For instance, when the time comes and you study Shakespeare, be sure to read his *Richard the Third.*"

"Shakespeare?"

"He was an Englishman who wrote plays."

"Why should I read that play, Grandpa?"

"Because he wrote about one of your kinsmen in that one, a man named Thomas Vaughan, who tutored King Edward's son."

"Oh," I said simply. That's all I could think to say, and then Granddad changed the subject. He got up from the swing, went back into our house, and asked if anyone wanted to go with him to see the stage show at the Van Lear theater. He had seen a billboard, advertising the coming appearance of a man who claimed to be Frank James, brother of the infamous Jesse James. Long thought dead, this man claimed he had escaped a henchman's bullet, and had been hiding out as someone named Joe Vaughan in western Arkansas. I heard Grandpa tell my dad that he and Frank were about the same age, which was 86, both having been born in 1848, and Grandpa said he thought he would know if the man was telling the truth since he had read a lot about both Frank and Jesse. But no one wanted to go see the man, neither my father, nor George, nor Ida Mae or my mother; no one but me. I said I would go.

Granddad didn't say anything. Instead, he continued to talk to my dad, hoping he would stop reading his newspaper, and get up from his rocking chair and go with him, but Dad remained seated. He just wasn't interested.

"I'll go, Grandpa," I repeated, pleading with him to take me along. Actually, I would go to any show, at any time, to see almost anything, but this sounded really special. Finally, my grandfather relented.

"All right, youngster," he said at last. "Let's go."

The interior of the theater on the second floor of the recreation building.

After sitting through a Tim McCoy western, the lights came on, and a handsomely dressed man appeared, and walked to the center of the small stage. He looked just like pictures that I had seen of Buffalo Bill Cody, all decked out in fringed buckskin jacket, tan hat, and boots, and he had a goatee just like Colonel Cody. Right away, I asked, "Is that him, Grandpa?"

Grandpa didn't say anything. The man on stage had yet to utter a word. Instead, he just stood there for the longest, staring down at us, almost elegant in his raiment, a really dramatic moment. Finally, he spoke.

"Good evening, ladies and gentlemen," he said, "My name is Frank James. Yes, I am THE Frank James, brother of the famous— some say infamous—Jesse James, the man who is said to have robbed banks and trains, the man killed in cold blood some years ago in Missouri."

The stage at the Van Lear theater, where my Grandfather and I saw "Frank James" in 1934. Pictured here is a "Tom Thumb Wedding" c. 1922, like the one my brother George once took part in.

"Is that him, Grandpa?" I asked, and Granddad told me to be quiet.

"As for myself," the man continued, "some have said that I too was gunned down shortly after my brother, but I am here to tell you that this is not so. I am here as living proof that it is a lie, the fabrication of a group of evil journalists."

"Is that him?" I asked, and Granddad once again told me to be quiet.

The old man continued with his story, spinning a yarn about how he, not Jesse, assumed the name of Joe Vaughan, and lived for years in northwest Arkansas, which was his present home.

"Joe Vaughan?" I asked, but Granddad ignored me.

As we walked home that night, I continued to nag at my grandfather, pestering him with the same questions, "Was that him? Was that the real Frank James?" And, "Who was Joe Vaughan?" But, Granddad remained silent until, finally, as we neared our house, he answered me.

"That wasn't Frank James," he said. "He told a good story, and a lot of it was true, but it wasn't Frank. Some years ago, Frank was shot at and hit in the leg, and after that he walked with a limp. That man told a good story, but he didn't walk with a limp." That was the end of that, and Grandpa never did explain why the man said what he said about Joe Vaughan. I guess Granddad never read anything about that.

Midterm has come. Time to turn in the semester themes. Maxine is called on to read hers first. "My family," she begins, "has been in eastern Kentucky a long, long time."

"Well, whose hasn't?," I can't help thinking.

"My father's family, the Sellards, were among the earliest settlers here," Maxine continues. "You have all probably heard about Jenny Wiley, and her capture and torture by the Indians. Well, she was a Sellards, her father was old Hezekiah Sellards, and that is the side of my family that has been here the longest."

After Maxine finished and sat down, Miss Hobson called on me, and I read my story. I told about old William marrying Fereby, his part-Cherokee lady, and a little more about his son, Thomas, then James, followed by Dad's dad, Anthony Wayne, my father, and then me and George and Ida Mae. I didn't say anything about the Vaughan place in Wales. I had learned very little about my mother's family, and I said so and then sat down.

Each of us turned in our written family stories, and awaited their return. Mine, which told only the barest of facts about the Vaughans and precious little about my mother's people, must have been too short, or not well done, as I got a B-grade for it, a real disappointment, but it made me resolve to be a better student, at least for the next week or so.

Shortly afterwards, something happened that would have an even greater effect on me than researching and writing my family theme. Miss Hobson read to us from her copy of Jesse Stuart's *Man with a Bull-Tongue Plow*, and I could almost see myself, "a farmer singing at the plow."

The Van Lear Baptist Church, scene of many colorful Christmas programs and other events that had a lasting effect on our young lives.

Christmas was our favorite time of the year. The Company gave out special Christmas baskets, there was usually snow on the ground, and the churches had Christmas pageants in which John Adams, Frankie Cunningham, and I often found ourselves decked out in bathrobes, playing the three wise men. Leo Perkowski was Joseph one year, after he started going to our Baptist Church and began sparking a pretty young girl named Lucille Walters. Church doings were fine, but it was all the toys that made it Christmas for most of us.

Not that we would get much stuff, but we always loved to go up to the Company's big store a week or two before the big day,

The main store at Van Lear where you could buy almost anything with U. S. currency or Consol scrip. Our favorite time was the Christmas season when we could see and wish for all sorts of things displayed in the store windows.

probably our favorite pre-Christmas ritual. There were two big windows full of stuff, all of it displayed on a backdrop of cotton snow, with miniature trees covered with icicles, and green and red garlands draped all over. I set my eye on an O-gauge train, circling the other toys, and I noticed that Richard had his eye on it too. Fat chance that either of us would get a train like that.

A week before Christmas, Dad roused me out of bed and asked me if I would like to go with him to get a Christmas tree. It took me about two seconds to say yes.

After I pulled on my overalls and a jacket, Mom insisted I wear my old flop-eared cap to keep my ears warm, so I put it on too. It wasn't real cold, but there was a chill in the air as we started out. Dad wore his favorite checked shirt and a green hunting cap, and carried his axe. This was rare for Dad. When he wasn't working in the mines, he usually was all decked out in coat, vest, and tie, and when he went uptown he always wore a hat, and sometimes spats. I asked Dad where we would go to get the tree.

"How 'bout Old Clubhouse Hill?" he said, coughing a hacky kind of cough, something he'd been doing quite a bit lately. "There's lots of good cedar trees there, where the first clubhouse and manager's house used to be. We should be able to find a dandy there.

"We'll walk the ridge down, and the railroad on the way back," Dad said, and he coughed again and hacked up some sputum, and I wondered if the coal dust he was always breathing had made his asthma worse.

We climbed the hill back of our house, and then walked atop the ridge until we reached the spot where we had built our kid's cabin. I proudly showed Dad what was left of our handiwork, which by now was only a shell of charred logs, the roof having burned and collapsed under its own weight. Dad was generous in his praise. "That must have been a fine cabin," he said. Some dads never ever said much to their sons or daughters, especially encouraging words like that. That's just the way it was.

While we rested from the climb, Dad started telling me some things about the hills in our part of Kentucky. During the millions of years that it had taken to form those hills, he said, masses of rich vegetation had been deposited, layer upon layer. "That's how the coal seams were formed," he said.

Where we boys had played just months ago, the garden of wild flowers that had bloomed was no more. Instead of vivid red and blue and purple and gold flowers, withered brown leaves now covered the ground. When we built our cabin, the hills were ablaze with color. Now, with the trees almost bare, we could look out for miles in every direction. We stood there for a long moment on the ridge, looking out over the valley and streams below. Off in the distance we could see John's Creek and its tributaries, following a twisted course that must have been laid out eons ago by those powerful glaciers that Miss Harris and Miss Hobson had told us about.

"It's a pretty sight," Dad said, and I quickly agreed. "You can almost see our pioneer ancestors when they first came here," he said.

I nodded, without speaking, enjoying that rare moment of camaraderie with my dad, while drinking in the tranquil wintry beauty of the scene. When we arrived at the old clubhouse site, Dad told me something about that place. "Two of the first buildings the Company built were the old club house and manager's house," he said, "and both were right here on this hill." He pointed to a spot where concrete pillars were still visible beneath the vegetation. "That was 1909, right after Consol bought the property," he continued. "There was a road up here and a board walk with maybe a hundred or more steps to it. A Mrs. Berlin was the first Club House manager, and I remember a Mary Dixon who worked there."

"What happened?" I asked

"The club house burned, and they lost the manager's house when they tried to move it down the hill, and the cables broke," Dad said.

Later that morning, we found a perfect Christmas tree, a big cedar, standing off to itself. After Dad chopped it down, he let me help him carry it home. I was proud as could be as we made our way down the hill, and walked back up town, along the railroad track, carrying the tree. That was a special moment for me, being with my father, sharing that day with him. I will never forget it.

Christmas morning finally came, and I got up real early and looked outdoors. There wasn't any snow on the ground like the year before, and that was a disappointment, but it was still Christmas, and something good was bound to happen. I remembered that Dad had said, even though I was getting older, a boy was never too old to have a new train, and so, with that good thought, I ran back into our living room, and there it was, sitting under the tree that Dad and I had cut. It wasn't a big Lionel—they cost too much—but it wasn't a windup toy either. All of my buddies had gotten little tin windup trains for Christmases past, with little-bitty circles of track and not much else. This train was an electric O-gauge with transformer and lots of track, and even a pair of switches and siding and a coal loader, just like the one we had seen in the commissary window. I stood there for a moment, just looking at it, and I said a little prayer of thanks even though I had never been what you would call religious.

I played with the train a while, switching from the main line to the siding, and loading and unloading the coal car, but this was too good to keep to myself, and so I went off to tell Richard about it and to see what he had got. It turned out his presents were a football, some money, a sled, and some books, which is what he said he wanted most of all, but I knew that he really wanted a train like mine, and so he put the books away, and we went back to our house and played with my train until supper time.

Christmas dinner was always something special. Mom cooked everything on our coal-fired kitchen stove, just like all the other Van Lear moms, and, even though I was responsible for getting in the kindling and coal, I never once thought about how hard those women labored to prepare our food. It was just a given, something they all did, without complaint. Never mind the heat and the cleaning up afterwards. All that we males were aware of was the good table they set before us, things like home-baked rolls, glistening with melted butter, egg-rich dumplings, turkey and oyster dressing, cranberries, and pumpkin pie, and sometimes even home-made ice cream. We had all of this and more this holiday. It was a good Christmas, even if it didn't snow.

That night, as I lay in my bed, I got to thinking about how good life was for me and for most of my friends in Van Lear. And I began to think about money, and how much things cost, and how hard most of the coal miners like my dad worked for their pay, which was a small amount for each ton of coal they loaded. Then I got to thinking about how little their pay was in relation to things they had to pay for, like house rent, for instance. Some of the mine foremen lived in houses larger than ours. I remember one of my friends, whose father was a foreman, saying that his dad had $8 held out of his pay every month for house rent. Our house rented for $4. The main store manager's house rented for $12. I didn't have any idea what the mine superintendent's house rented for, but it probably was $20 or more a month, an unimaginable sum to me. The miners had their rent deducted from their paychecks, along with other expenses. Coal was a dollar a ton, delivered to the renter's coal house. Insurance was three dollars; electricity usually was a dollar or two; union dues, a dollar and a half; lamp rental, another dollar; and, if you had drawn any scrip, that too was deducted. I had heard Dad tell Mom that his take-home pay for the week before Christmas wouldn't be more than ten or twenty dollars. Time was when a miner's pay was much more, but when things got slow, expenses remained high. Dad had probably spent half of his take-home pay on my train, and the other half on food for our table. While I lay there that night, I thought about all of this—the miners' life, how hard they worked for their pay and all—and it sent a chill down my spine. This made me sad, but I finally turned my thoughts to being thankful for the special dinner we had, and all the other blessings in Van Lear. Soon I was fast asleep, dreaming of things kids dreamed about back in those days, like next spring and baseball games.

Before the year ended, the St. Louis Cardinals won the National League pennant and the World Series, Max Baer became the world's heavyweight boxing champion, the New York Giants were NFL pro football champs, and Snail Lambert and Otchel Daniels were the two athletes that Richard and I most admired in Van Lear and Johnson County, Kentucky.

Spring came and went, but not before we fourth-grade boys were called on to endure the embarrassment of taking part in the May Day Maypole dance, a ritual established years ago by Miss Clara Shaw, who thought that every child should participate in such things. The Maypole dance was performed around a tall pole which had been decorated with a couple of dozen crepe paper streamers, twisted into fancy curlicues. Stretched out some twelve to twenty feet from the pole, each colored streamer was held by a young student, girl, boy, girl, boy, and so forth. There would be music from some teacher's wind-up phonograph, and we would dance around the Maypole, skipping along, merrily singing words to a song that

I can no longer remember. Our reprieve from this gross insult occurred none too soon when we were all herded down to the football field for the day's recreational competitions. These events included sack and potato races, three-legged races, and the like, and I always did well in all except the latter, in which Worth or Marcus would be my three-legged partner, and we were never able to get our two lashed-together legs functioning as one. After the awarding of blue ribbons, we were herded back to school. The next day, Doctor Wolfe set up his dental chair and examined our teeth in the first-grade room. I can still recall the not unpleasant odor of his pipe, and his gentle monotone as he dictated his findings to his nurse: "No calculus, no stain..." I wonder if dentists still do and say things like that.

The tipple at Van Lear Mine No. 155 as it appeared on that fateful July day in 1935. Coal came up from the opening ramp and was sent to the tipple to be washed and sorted. The men entered the mine through another opening, not visible beyond this structure. Further east, a third opening provided ventilation via a fan and air shaft.

Chapter Four
The Accident

To the living we owe respect,
but to the dead we owe only the truth.
—*Voltaire*

The year was 1935, early evening, a little over two weeks after another big baseball game and Fourth of July celebration. We were all in bed, but not asleep, when I heard a rap at our front door. Dad got up and went to the door. It was Buster Franklin, Galen Franklin's son. I heard him say that his dad was sick and couldn't work. Would Dad like to work in his place? Work was still slack, and Dad said he would be glad to work in Galen's place. He would be working with a small crew, pulling track in an abandoned section of the mine, while the rest of the mine was idle, except for a pumper and a motorman or two. I soon went to sleep.

I always wondered what happened the next morning. The following is my version of what *might* have occurred.

The next morning, Jim Vaughan was up and out of the house early. He caught a ride with the Kretzers to the mine, and went straight to the bath house, where he put on his working clothes, placed his street clothes in the basket on the chain hoist, reeled it up to hang alongside other miners' clothes under the high ceiling, closed the padlock, and walked over to the lamp house to check out a headlamp and freshly charged battery. He was busy, strapping the battery onto his big leather belt, when the shift foreman told him that his working buddies that day would be brothers Charley and

Bill Kretzer with whom he had ridden to work, Frank Tuzy, Roy Murray, Sherley Hereford, Honus Gool, Durward Litz, and Virgil Clay. Of the nine men in the track-pulling crew, Jim Vaughan was the oldest at 53, and Virgil Clay the youngest. He was 21. The shift foreman had brought good news. He knew all of these men, and although Virgil was quite young he was said to be a good and careful worker. Safety was the watchword at Van Lear. The miners practiced it daily, and even had special safety meets, where they competed with other mining communities in demonstrations of safe mining practices.

Jim Vaughan walked outside and joined his fellow workers aboard the two cars that made up the mantrip. Since there were only the nine of them, they would not need more cars. A minute later they were descending the slope at the main driftmouth of the mine, a ritual they had done over and over, usually accompanied by a hundred or more other miners, always in darkness, except for the dim glow of a string of overhead lightbulbs, and usually in total silence. The temperature dropped almost immediately, first from the eighty-degree level at the surface to sixty degrees, where it would remain throughout the workday. The constant coolness, aided and abetted by the fan-generated breeze of fresh air, was one of the few features of underground coal mining that could be described as enjoyable, especially on hot and sweltering summer days. Even the water dripping from the roof, and the hollow echo of mining sounds were pleasant to the ear. The work itself and the ever-present danger attendant to it were something else.

The grinding sound of the windlass stopped as the cars reached the bottom of the slope, and the motorcar took over the job of pulling the cars. The top of the electric motorcar measured a scant two feet above the floor, allowing it to squeeze itself under the lowest ceilings of the mine's interior rooms and entries. The motorman would deliver the men to the entry near the place where they were to work, a hundred feet beneath the surface, and more than a mile farther into the mine. As they rocked along in total darkness, the

tram lurched occasionally as the motorman varied its speed by turning a big wheel connected to a rheostat, the uneven rails causing
sparks to fly from the overhead wire. Occasionally, the front end of
the motorcar would bump into an air-door, a device which allowed
air to exit the main tunnel through a shoefly, a forty-five degree
crossover connecting the hallway with the main airway, the con-
duit used to draw outside air through the bowels of the mine from
a huge motor-driven fan.

*This photo from Jim Cook's collection shows miners gathered near Mine No. 151. In this group are Con
Daniels, Bill Kretzer, Jack Adams, Emmett Grove, George Davis, Melvin Music, Bill Dixon, Jim Bob Worland,
Sheridan Gibbs, Roy Lee, Jay Phelps, Jim Music, Curtis Barbour, Lawrence Meddings, and Bob Jasper.*

When they reached a spot designated on the engineers' map as
first-right, the small workcrew got off the tram. With their dinner
pails, cables, pry bars, and other paraphernalia in hand, they began
the walk toward their workplace, although walk was not really what
they did. Duck-waddle would be a more apt description. Bent at
the waist to avoid scraping their backs on the low ceiling, they stayed
in this strained position for another hundred yards, arriving finally
at the face of the entry. There, they dropped to their knees, thankful

Four miners, John Sotnikoff, Charlie Bell, Miltie Castle, and Marion Ward, emerge from the driftmouth of Mine No. 155 around 1940.

to be able to relieve the tension on their backs, but destined to remain bent over for the remainder of their workday. In this they were far from unique. All eastern Kentucky miners, save a few in the Garrett and Elkhorn Creek coal fields, spent most of their working lives on their knees, their backs up against a ceiling of rock and slate.

An ordinary workday in the Van Lear mine for most coal loaders meant that, during the preceding work shift, a "cutter" had undercut the face of the coal to be mined, thus relieving the coal loader of that particular chore. Mining a "place" meant boring holes, tamping explosives in the holes, capping each charge with a percussion cap, and stringing and lighting long fuses to set off the blast. After retreating a safe distance, the miner would yell out three times: "Fire in the hole!" And then he would light the fuse. If the holes had been well-placed, and if the face had been cleanly undercut, the ensuing explosion broke the face into loadable chunks of coal, ranging in size from dust to huge lumps that would require the efforts of two men to load them into a mine car. Often, these lumps were so big and blocky, there would be insufficient room between the top of the car and the roof of the mine to load them, and it would be necessary for the miner to use his pick to break them into smaller pieces to render them loadable. Ordinary, everyday mining was dangerous, but not nearly so dangerous as pillar-pulling when the miners attempted to blast and remove the one huge pillar remaining in a section, and then load as much coal as they could without endangering their lives. Once the pillar was pulled, that part of the mountain would drop, and there would be no further mining in that section, at least from that seam of coal. On this particular day, there would be no blasting, pillar-pulling, or coal-loading, only the fairly simple procedure of removing and salvaging the rails. Still, there was potential danger. There was methane gas in the Miller's Creek coal field, and under the right conditions it could be explosive! All of the miners were well aware of possible danger. Jim Vaughan and Frank Tuzy knew that the floor of first-right had begun to swell and heave so much that the rooms

Jim Vaughan with two young boys and his daughter Ida Mae, c. 1924.

there had to be abandoned. That upward swelling was a sure sign of gas pressure from below, and the swelling extended all the way from the entry into the airway. The men had been directed to go there while sufficient room remained between the floor and the roof to pull and save the valuable steel rails.

Frank Tuzy with daughters Thelma and Agnes.

Before commencing their work, Jim and Frank crawled around the entry, poking a shortened spad into the ceiling, sounding it out for possible fractures. Each of them took turns, tapping every foot along the overhead roof, while listening for hollow sounds that would indicate loose slate. The roof appeared to be sound. Meanwhile, the other men laid out cables which they would use to pull the rails out of the swollen area, once they were set free from their ties. They crawled to the side of the entry, sat down next to their dinner pails, and watched while their working buddies completed their jobs, the bobbing lights from their lamps painting moving yellow patterns across the glistening black coal. One last chore remained. Frank began to crawl around the darkened room once more. This time, he turned his head from side to side, allowing his headlamp to illuminate the supporting timbers that helped hold up the roof. When he came to a timber, he hit it with the heal of his gloved hand to test its soundness. Some of the timbers were no more than three feet high where the roof and floor had squeezed almost together, so low he could scarcely wriggle beneath. Jim looked at his pocket watch. It was 8:30. Frank rejoined him, and the nine-man crew set about the job of saving the track.

James Young crossed the railroad track and Miller's Creek bridge, and breathlessly ran down the main road to our part of town. "Did'ja hear about it?" he yelled out when he found me sitting on the front steps of our house. "There's been an explosion at the mine," James said, still gasping for air, "and your dad is in it!"

I stood up, speechless, all sorts of thoughts now racing through my mind. I recalled last night, Buster Franklin's visit, Dad's working in Galen Franklin's place, and then I thought about how safe the mines had always been. There had been accidents, but no one that I knew of had died in Consol's Van Lear mines.

"I just heard about it up at the store," James said, still out of breath. He ran on down the road, and I sat there for a moment, staring after him.

When I went inside our house I knew immediately that my mother had already heard the news. She was sitting at the kitchen table, a worried look on her face. She grabbed and hugged me, and began to cry, which made me think all sorts of bad things had happened to Dad, but then she realized what she had done, and she hugged me again even tighter and said, "Maybe your father will be all right, son. He's such a good man, and a good miner. And I have faith that God won't let him die. But, pray for him, son, and for the others."

I nodded and went outside. People were walking, some running, toward midtown, and I heard one of them say, "Those men will never get out of there alive." And then another answered, "They say the whole section is sealed off by a heavy slatefall. There's no way they can be alive."

I started walking up the hillside. Of all the things you could turn to for solace at a time like this, the hills would be the thing that would most likely ease your pain. All of us Van Lear boys knew that, although I don't think we ever talked about it. There had been a lot of rain, and the Cumberland foothills of the Appalachians were really pretty that summer. As I walked along, heavy hearted, I reached a plateau, a place with big wild grape vines, and it was then that I realized that this was the spot Richard had picked to build our tree house, the place where we found the nest of copperhead snakes. And then I remembered, it was less than a year ago, near this very spot, that we had all looked into the long, narrow slit, and argued about what had caused it. I remembered how Richard had explained that the slits occurred when the miners pulled the last pillars of coal, and the mountain fell. I got up and went to the slit and stood there, and then I kneeled and looked down into that black hole in the ground.

"Hello...hello...hello." I could still hear the calls echoing back as I knelt there. Then, suddenly, I had this strange idea, only it didn't seem so strange to me. Perhaps what I had been told was only a dream—a nightmare!—perhaps Dad hadn't been in a mine explosion after all. That was what I told myself. It had to be! Soon my dad, Jim Vaughan himself—a living, breathing man—would come climbing out of that mine, right through that very slit in the hilltop, and Frank Tuzy and Virgil Clay and all those other miners would be with him, and the nine of them would be all black and grimy, but they would be alive.

Although I had never been inside the mine where the explosion occurred, my dad had taken me a short distance beyond the mouth of old Mine No. 151, and the memory of that event came back to me. It was late one Saturday afternoon when the mine wasn't "working." Dad and a small crew had been hired to close that mine, and

Mine No. 151 tipple and rail cars.

A ten-ton electric locomotive like the one my father used to take me inside Mine No. 151 before closing it in 1931.

when he came home for lunch, I had begged him to take me back into the mine before he closed it, and I remembered how my Mom protested, but finally agreed that I could go. I remembered mounting the motorcar and sitting next to Dad, and then he put the big steel machine in motion. In my mind I could now recall that day clearly—how cool the air felt on my face and hands; how the motorcar made a thump, thump sound as it hit the doors at the airway intersections; how the electric arc from the trolley tram wire smelled; how the pale yellow headlight illuminated the black walls of the shaft; how Dad had told me to sit quietly and not reach out or stick my leg outside the confines of the motorcar; how he announced mine landmarks as we passed them, entries driven left and right off the main hallway and airway, 2 West, 3 East, and then 1 North; and how safe I felt there in that potentially lethal hole in the ground.

I sat there for a long moment, and tried hard to remember all the good things, especially about how safe the Van Lear mines were.

I looked up, searching for a familiar face, a live face, the face of my father. There was no one there, and I'm sure my face now reflected my deep pain. The accident hadn't been a dream. It had been real. And nothing would change that. I didn't go on around the hill to our old cabin site as we had done the day Dad and I went off to find our Christmas tree. Instead, I went back down the hillside. By the time I got back to our house, a steady stream of cars filled the main road, all of them headed east toward the mine. Mrs. O'Bryan and Mrs. Sparks and some other neighborhood women were there, trying to comfort my mother. My brother George had gone to the mine. I vaguely recall this. All other recollections from that day and the next three are dim and hazy, at best.

Dad's brother, Everett (Sook) Vaughan, was a federal mine inspector, then living with his family in Pikeville. When the news of the accident reached him, he drove the winding and treacherous 37 miles along Highway 23 in something under forty minutes, arriving at the Van Lear mine just as they were removing the first of the nine bodies. When the mine officials learned that his brother was one of the nine, they refused to allow Uncle Everett to enter the mine. My brother George was also restrained from joining the rescue party.

Everett Vaughan, third from the right in this pre-1920 photo, was employed as a federal mine inspector in 1935. One of the first to reach the scene of the Van Lear accident, rescue workers barred him from entering the mine when they learned that his brother Jim was one of the nine entrapped miners. Their brother John is pictured, third from the left.

In time, all nine bodies were recovered, and their families buried them—the Kretzers in their family cemetery at Reedsville, near Hitchins in Carter County; Virgil Clay in a cemetery on Richmond Hill at Van Lear; Roy Murray in his family's cemetery plot near Lowmansville; Durward Litz in a cemetery near Auxier and East Point, across the river from Harman Station; Honus Gool at the mouth of Webb Hollow in Van Lear; Sherley Hereford in Ashland Cemetery; Frank Tuzy in Mayo Cemetery at Paintsville; and my father, Jim Vaughan, at Rose Hill in Ashland. W.K. Wood, pastor of Pollard Baptist Church and long-time friend of our family, officiated at Dad's funeral service. I recall that our first viewing of my father's lifeless remains left all of us feeling that the face looked nothing like him. Before his burial, Lazear Funeral Home made a special effort to re-create my father's facial features, and the result was more natural.

All Hope For Other 2 Men Abandoned

Miners Died Instantly From Gas, Daniels Says

ASHLAND MAN IS VICTIM

James E. Vaughn, Among The Miners Killed Yesterday

July 17 1935

By W. F. ARBOGAST
Associated Press Staff Writer

VAN LEAR, Ky., July 18. (P)— Seven of the nine men entombed by a coal mine explosion here yesterday were found dead by rescue workers today, and all hope was abandoned for the other two.

The bodies were brought to the surface, one by one, in mine railway cars this morning.

John F. Daniel, Lexington, chief of the state department of mines and minerals, expressed belief that all nine had been killed instantly by gas.

Some of the bodies had been crushed by falling slate and coal. All were brought to undertaking establishments in Van Lear.

Frank Price, chief clerk for the Consolidation Coal Company, whose mine No. 5 was the scene of the disaster, said the bodies recovered were those of William Kretzler, 41, assistant foreman; Charles Kretzler, 46; Virgil Clay, 21; James E. Vaughan, 52; Derwood Litz, 34; Sherley Hereford, 38; and Roy Murray, 38.

JAMES VAUGHN IS VICTIM OF BLAST

James Vaughn, 52, whose lifeless body this morning was recovered from the No. 5 mine of the Consolidation Coal Co. at Van Lear, Ky., where he was trapped in an explosion yesterday, will be buried in Rose Hill cemetery here tomorrow afternoon.

Mr. Vaughn, who is the father of three children, lived here until about ten years ago and was well known in this city.

Funeral service will be conducted from the Pollard Baptist Church tomorrow afternoon at three o'clock with Rev. W. K. Wood in charge. The body today was removed to a Paintsville undertaker's establishment and will be brought to Ashland tomorrow.

He leaves his wife and three children at Van Lear; his father, Wayne Vaughn of Ashland; one sister, Mrs. R. M. Ball of Sixth street, Pollard; and three brothers, Edward of Van Lear and Howard and Toby of Ashland. He also is survived by many other relatives. His father and brother Toby make their home with Mrs. Ball.

After hearing news of the tragic accident yesterday the relatives here had waited with dwindling hope that Mr. Vaughn might be found alive. That faint hope was taken away this morning when

Newspaper clippings with stories of the 1935 Van Lear mine disaster, which took the lives of nine men, including the fathers of the six Kretzer children pictured in the center.

A report issued by the Bureau of Mines summed up the matter in plain language. It stated, "The mine (#155) had two shallow slopes and an airshaft, and was connected to Number 154 mine. At 8:40 A.M., men on a locomotive, approaching first-right, felt a heavy concussion and, after looking into the mouth of first-right, they telephoned outside that an explosion had occurred.

"Calls for assistance were sent to the state mine inspector, the company offices at Jenkins, Kentucky, other mines, and the Norton Station of the Bureau of Mines. Crews and rescue leaders arrived promptly.

"Ventilation was advanced by erecting brattices and curtains. Progress was impeded by roof falls, especially where timbers were knocked down or broken in the squeezed area. A gas-mask crew explored ahead of the brattice men, and an apparatus crew made one trip to look for a possible fire, but none was found. The bodies were removed by July 19, two from under heavy falls.

"Gas had accumulated in the squeezing rooms in which ventilation was almost cut off; it moved onto the entry where it was ignited by an arc from the wiring of a motor or a pump. An open-type electric locomotive nearby was not in operation. The explosion picked up and ignited a small amount of coal dust, but did not propagate out of the immediate section.

"The mine was not rock-dusted, but dust on the entries contained material from the clay floor and brushed roof. The bodies were burned, broken, and crushed. Electric cap lamps were used, but the mine was not considered gassy."

Whatever the cause—and it was never fully established or documented—apparently all nine men died instantly from the concussion of the blast and the ensuing slate and rock fall. News of the disaster spread quickly and occupied the attention of the nation for a full week. It was one of the worst disasters ever to occur in the eastern Kentucky coal field.

Van Lear never seemed the same after that tragedy. Although I had been comforted somewhat by the beauty of the hills the day of the accident, nothing could lessen my grief for very long. Until the moment of my fathers' death, my life had been happy and carefree. It had

O.D. Sparks and George W. Vaughan (both VLHS 1932) c. 1935.

never occurred to me that my dad could one day be taken from me, certainly not like this and so soon. We were all young and innocent, full of life, busy experiencing all the great and wonderful things that our town had given us. In our minds, we were immortal—even our parents—and, although we had serious moments when logic told us that there would be sad times, that was not a part of the present, the here and now, only something in the far distant future. And as for death, well, that happened to others, not to us or ours, not to me.

Time dulls the pain of loss, fortunately, and there were good people at Van Lear who helped us. George's friends, Lowell Phillips, Deward Kazee, Harold Rucker, Edgar Stapleton, Earl Anderson, O.D. Sparks, and Erwin Brown rallied to his side following our father's death. I spent a lot of time with Uncle Everett and Aunt Maude, and their sons, Gene, Warren, and Maurice, first at their home on the banks of the Big Sandy at Pikeville, and later at Martin in nearby

Warren, Gene, Aunt Maude, Charlene, and Maurice Vaughan, c. 1935.

Floyd County. Aunt Maude, Uncle Everett, Charlene, Gene, Warren, and Maurice made me part of their family and diverted me from some of the memories of the previous weeks, but most of the time I was in a kind of fog. We took part in all sorts of sports. I recall sparring with Gene and Warren, and getting knocked on my rear, and it was things like this that helped me back to a sense of reality.

The Van Lear miners had always opposed unions for the most part, feeling that as long as the Company looked after them, there was no need for one, and there probably wasn't, because everyone readily acknowledged that Consolidation Coal Company had been good to their workers, but they finally voted for the union anyway.

This steel tipple replaced the old wooden tipple at Mine No. 155 a few years after the accident. All production from mines 4 and 5 was then funneled through this facility.

The year after the explosion, Consol built a new steel tipple at Mine No. 155, and all of the mining operations at Van Lear were consolidated into a single processing plant. Despite this and a few other improvements, it soon became clear that Van Lear's days as an important coal-mining entity were numbered.

I had always wondered why my father had elected to endure

the dangers always present in a coal mine. After all, he had other options, and I knew that the coal miner's earnings had declined. I recalled that he said he felt better in a mine, where the temperature was always cool, but that didn't satisfy my curiosity. Most Van Lear miners loaded sixteen to twenty or more tons of coal in an eight-hour day. I recalled that three years earlier, in 1932, Dad and George talked about their wages. At that time, the coal-loader's wage ranged from 50 to 65 cents a ton, and a good loader could earn from $125 to $200 every two weeks, but I also knew that with coal prices low and the mines only working a few days a week, the miners hadn't been earning nearly as much for the past two years.

My father always kept accurate account books, whether operating a small mine as he once did in partnership with his father, or when working for a company like Consol, either as a coal loader, a foreman, or by the hour, as he was doing at the time of his death. I found his account book, and opened it to the final page. My mother had added one final entry: "Killed on this day, July 15, 1935. Gas mine explosion." The error in the date was hers, as the fifteenth of July was a Monday, and the fatal explosion was on a Wednesday. I turned to an earlier page and found the following entries that Dad had made for two weeks in October of 1934, the fifth year of the Great Depression:

Two weeks' take-home pay, October 16-31, 1934:

84 hours		$55.20
Less Withholding		19.08
Insurance	3.28	
Scrip	4.00	
Rent	4.00	
Doctor/Hosp.	1.25	
Electricity	2.00	
Coal/Hauling	1.97	
Lamp	.96	
Sales Tax	.12	
Union Dues	1.50	
Net Payroll		$36.12

This accounting was for a two-week period, in a year in which my father had taken a job as a day laborer, following an injury to his back. Had he been able to continue that year as a coal loader, he would have earned a bit more, or if he had resumed work as a section foreman, still more, but not a great deal more. All Van Lear coal was hand loaded, and the miner who loaded it for that same two-week period in October of 1934 may have earned a gross income of $61.25 instead of $55.20, providing he hand-loaded 175 tons during those two weeks, and providing he was paid 35 cents a ton to load it. As I thought about all this, my resolve to never work in the mines became more fixed.

Life went on for all of us who had been directly affected by the tragic events. My brother George, who had dropped out of high school to work for a year in 1931, had returned to school and had graduated with the class of 1932. He had resumed his work in the mines the following year. After the death of our father, he worked outside the mines for a time and gave some thought to accepting a partial scholarship to an electrical engineering school. Instead, he returned to work in the mines and remained in Van Lear,

My brother George Vaughan was principal "breadwinner" for our family after our father's death until his induction into the army in 1941.

helping my mother and me and our sister, who was in nurses' training in Covington.

For me and my peers Van Lear was a place where there were always things to do, and adults to help us do them. Although our parents were supportive, I don't recall that the older folk interfered with our day-to-day routines. There were activities like the Campfire Girls, organized during the early years by Clara Shaw, Boy Scouts led by Herman Pack, Lyceum programs arranged by the theater manager, safety meets and ball games sponsored by the Company, and all sorts of church and school-sponsored activities. But programs like the town orchestra and choir of the 1920s had ended, and the visiting bands from Cincinnati and elaborate stage shows were becoming less frequent. Despite our fondest hopes for our beloved coal town, even Richard and I were aware that the best days of old Van Lear, if not already behind her in 1935, soon would be.

Chapter Five
Life Goes On

Teach us delight in simple things,
And mirth that has no bitter springs;
Forgiveness free of evil done,
And love to all men 'neath the sun!
—The Children's Song

A year after the accident, George bought a new 1936 two-door Plymouth sedan for $570, loaded us up, and took us to Flint, Michigan to visit Mom's sister, Aunt Mayme and her husband Uncle Bill Howell. All five of their sons had good jobs in the auto industry in and around Flint, and Harry and Ray had nice cabins on Sage Lake, where we spent a week catching blue gill and enjoying the cooler northern breezes. Upon our return to Kentucky, I made up my mind that I would one day get a good education and find work like my Howell cousins and, eventually, a wife as pretty as Ray's wife, Irene.

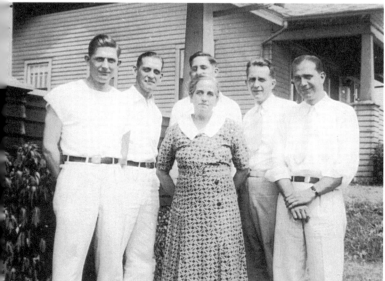

Aunt Mayme Howell and her sons, Ray, Willard, Chet, Harry, and Leonard. Harry and Ray hosted our visit to their cabins on Sage Lake north of Flint, Michigan in the summer of 1936. Mom's sisters, Aunt Mayme and Aunt Min, helped see me through my senior year at Ashland Senior High School. Harry and Wynne Howell then took me under their wing prior to my entry into the Navy V-5 flight program in 1943.

Soon after we arrived back home, I awoke early one morning with a razor-sharp pain in my midsection, and they rushed me over to Paintsville Hospital where Doctor Aiken removed my ruptured appendix. When I complained about the long, ugly scar, the good doctor explained that I was lucky to be alive, and I griped no more.

To relieve the tedium of sitting around while my belly healed, I dug through our small cache of books and happened upon the Ashland book that Dad had bought for me on that train trip three years ago. As I scanned the pages, I relearned some of the things that I had forgotten about Ashland, triggering more memories of some of the town's early leaders, and my own family as well. I read once more about Martin Tobey Hilton, the engineer who came to Catlettsburg in 1853 to establish the eastern terminus of a new Lexington & Big Sandy Railroad. That was twenty-seven years before the Chesapeake and Ohio Railroad came to town. At that time, pig iron was being produced west of Ashland in places like Princess and Star Furnace, and it was the owners of these small industries, along with Kentucky Iron, Coal & Manufacturing Company, who urged the location of the new rail line at Poage's Landing, or Poage's Settlement as some had called it, the little hamlet on the river that would later be renamed Ashland. The iron furnaces and coal mines must have been the reason my mother's father came to Kilgore to set up his blacksmith shop. The small furnaces and coal mines no longer exist, not even a trace of them. Several members of our family, including my Aunt Min and Uncle Crockett, Aunt Kate and Uncle Ernest, and Aunt Bryda and Uncle Lewis, moved into Ashland to find jobs in the steel and rail industries. Aunt Min took work as a telephone operator. As I reread the little book, I recalled that it was Mister Hilton who laid out the city of Ashland, and provided space for those wide boulevards and for what would later become Central Park. But the book had little to say about J.C.C. Mayo, the man responsible for the building of my town. I still wanted to know more about him.

Following my recovery from the appendectomy, I was soon able to rejoin my buddies, riding bicycles and doing most of the things everyone else was doing. Before school started, however, my friend and neighbor Bobby Gunning lost his mother, and my mother had him come to our house to live with us while his father got their lives back together. Bobby and I spent a lot of time that fall, sitting together on the railroad, throwing ballast rocks, and talking about all sorts of things. During some of these gab sessions we compared notes about towns we had visited. I told him about Ashland, and he told me about Closplint and Jenkins.

I can't be certain that some of my youthful indiscretions didn't play a role in my mother's decision to let me go to Baptist camp at Clear Creek near Pine Mountain a couple of weeks after I was released from the hospital. She may have felt that a kid who would spend his brother's hard-earned dollar for a twelve-pound sack of candy and not volunteer to share it with others probably stood in need of divine intervention. At any rate, I went to church camp, along with Walter and Bill Cassell, and it was during one of the vespers services that I felt called on to publicly declare my faith and become a Christian. I wrote a card to my mother and brother telling them about this, and a week later I was baptized by Reverend Curl in the little baptistery at our Van Lear Missionary Baptist Church.

My mother and her Sunday School class at Van Lear Baptist Church, c. 1940. Pictured in the top row are Louise King (VLHS 1945) at the far right, and Peggy Beers (VLHS 1945), fifth from right. Doris Ann Harris (VLHS 1944) is the middle girl in the front row.

No one told me that I would be called on to offer up a public prayer, but on the Sunday following my immersion, that is what occurred during morning services. I was caught totally unprepared, and being a mere lad, I saw no need to respond. For the most part, my prayers continue to be silent and private.

Despite the good influence of a church and parents, we youngsters continued to live life on the edge when on our own, which was most of our waking hours. Although we were only twelve or thirteen years of age, we often joined the older boys in antics that sometimes bordered on being downright dangerous and perhaps even illegal. For instance, until they tore down the old Number 1 tipple and mine tracks and removed the mine cars, we would push one of the cars to the old mine entrance and then coast in it to the tipple, or else switch it to a siding and coast back toward the old fan house.

On Halloween in 1937 we were out at dusk, playing a game which we called "Whistle or Holler." In this game, one person was "it" and had to find the other players, who hid out in corn fodder shocks, in ditches, or wherever they could find a good hiding place. When the "it" person yelled out, "Whistle or holler," the hidden players had to whistle or holler to give the "it" person a clue as to their whereabouts. Billy had just discovered me, when we heard a commotion coming down the road. A group of older boys were out playing pranks, so we joined them. One of the first things the gang did was move a footbridge over the creek at the old Number 1 mine. We watched this and then went along with them toward Bradley Crossing. When we reached the little house that newly-weds Tubby and Carrie Cecil Harris lived in, two of the boys started turning over their outhouse, whereupon Tubby came running outside, and commenced pleading with them. "Boys," he said, "I don't mind you doing your pranks, but please don't turn the outhouse over. Carrie's inside!" We went on our way, never knowing if she was or wasn't.

The next summer our Boy Scout troop reorganized, and we went on two camping trips, the first to Fish Trap on Paint Creek and the second to Camp Arrowhead, in West Virginia. Upon our return home, Richard learned that we could wangle a place on the 4-H livestock team by learning to judge chickens, which both of our families kept for meat and eggs, and we did just that, somehow earning a place on the ag-agent's judging team from Johnson County. Our trip to Louisville and the Kentucky State Fair earned us no blue ribbons, but we did get a couple of second-place awards, and we returned home with some knowledge of how to recognize a healthy vent on an adult mother hen.

Elizabeth Wheatley.

The years passed rather quickly. Soon, we were sitting in Elizabeth Wheatley's eighth grade, where that lovely lady taught us the regular bill of fare—English grammar, literature, history, math, and science—and music and drawing as well. I had always thought that I could sing, but I was in for a surprise when I was not included in Miss Wheatley's choral group. And, there was another let-down. I had always liked to draw, and I thought I had some talent along those lines, but I soon learned that Charles Bowling and Lawrence Young could out-draw me and anyone else in our class. I did receive the class scholarship medal, and was named valedictorian at year's end. So I guess I did some things right.

The next summer, my sister Ida Mae invited me to visit her in Covington, across the Ohio River from Cincinnati. She had an apartment near Saint Elizabeth's Hospital where she now worked as a registered nurse. Richard's brother O.D. Sparks and his wife had sublet rooms at my sister's place while he interned at Saint Elizabeth's, and they were moving to a new mining town in eastern Kentucky, where he would be the company doctor. I had a good time that week, walking across Suspension Bridge to Fountain

Square, gawking at Carew Tower and the other tall buildings, and recalling the excursion trip during the train ride to and from Cincinnati.

When I returned home I amused myself by hooking up a doorbell to our company house, but when the construction foreman found out about it, he made me remove it. My mother, noticing my restlessness and sensing a need to get me involved in some worthwhile endeavor, suggested that I do something other than use her

Ida Mae Vaughan (VLHS 1935) c. 1939.

electric iron as a hotplate. I had learned that by turning it upside down and placing the handle in a vise-like grip, I could set a pan on it and make fudge. When I said that I would like to learn to develop and print photos, she said that she would pay half the cost of a developer kit if I could pay the other half, which I soon earned by helping Richard clean out the mule barn once more. After mastering the developing and printing process, I felt that I was ready to learn to make enlargements, but again I lacked the necessary cash. My mother then gave me her old Kodak Brownie box camera, which I converted into an enlarger by attaching it to a vertical pole on a wooden base. Because of these and other such experiences, my later exposure to physics courses and optics and light would have an air of familiarity.

Before the next school year began, we had another summer of fun. It was during the final week of that vacation that Richard and I resurrected *The Gazette*. The reason we cranked up the paper again had to do with the last baseball game of the season. Van Lear had some outstanding baseball teams, both the varsity teams representing the high school and the independent teams put together and managed by Emmett Lambert. The local people were loyal fans, and over the years they had been aided and abetted at every turn by Jack Price, a mine superintendent who dearly loved baseball, and by the superintendents who followed him and carried on that tradition. Whenever the Van Lear town team had a weakness, like needing a good relief pitcher, the Super would help by providing a job in the mines for any young man who had a good curveball. On occasion, Van Lear patrons of baseball even paid a moundsman of known ability to come from some distant town to pitch for their beloved team, especially when winning a particular game was in doubt.

Leonard Meade and Tony Clifton (both VLHS 1943), USMC, in 1944, several years after Tony stole home and Richard and I wrote a poem about his feat and published it in our Van Lear Gazette.

Over the years the Van Lear town teams played all up and down the Big Sandy Valley with great success against other coal-town teams, but they always took special delight in defeating their county seat rivals from Paintsville. This year the town team had a perfect record, except for an early-season loss to Paintsville, and they were to face that same team in their last game of the season. To celebrate the event, our town had a big blowout with a bicycle parade, followed by free slices of iced watermelon and bottles of soda pop, climaxed by the baseball game that afternoon and fireworks that night. Our friend Tony was slick enough with his glove to get a uniform and sit on the bench as the Bankmules' utility infielder, and now he was dressed out, although he probably wouldn't get to play unless the game was a runaway.

Before the game, there was the bicycle parade and judging. Tony sat on the bench alongside the older players, and watched the rest of us younger boys circle the infield on bikes that we had decorated with crepe paper. With the paper rustling and flying in the breeze, all of us were feeling kind of silly, and we tried to show off by doing a lot of fancy pedaling, especially Clifford Honaker, who could steer his bike without even touching the handlebars. Just when we thought that Clifford had won the bike event, some little kid from John's Creek was declared the winner. We then stowed our two-wheelers, grabbed a peach Nehi, and claimed seats in back of the players along the firstbase line, glad to have the bicycle embarrassment behind us.

"Who's on first?" I asked Richard, who had volunteered to help the official scorer keep the team's scorebook.

"Butcher," he said, and I asked which Butcher. There were three older Butcher boys, all of them good baseball players, and all of them were suited up.

"Junior," he answered. "Junior Butcher's on first, Pat McCoart's on second, Troy Thacker's at short, and Paul Butcher's on third."

"Two ?" I asked, rolling my eyes. "Two Butchers in the infield?"

Billy, who was looking over Richard's shoulder, agreed. "Oh no!"

he moaned. "A two-Butcher infield sounds like a bush-league team." In addition to Paul and Junior, their younger brother Danny was playing right field, and we all knew that a real team wouldn't have that many players from one family. Even Richard nodded in agreement, but he didn't say anything since he was helping the scorekeeper. All of us were mightily influenced by the pro teams, and except for Lloyd and Paul Waner—Big Poison and Little Poison—the three DiMaggios and the Dean brothers, there were few families with more than one player in the major leagues, much less three on one team. But, in all fairness, the Butchers were exceptional athletes. We all admitted that.

After Emmett conferred with the homeplate umpire—there were two more umps for the bases, which meant this really was a special game—he came back to the bench and spoke to his son Snail, and then Snail got up and walked to the warmup alley in back of first base and began to pitch to the Bankmules' catcher Ab Daniels. This could mean only one thing: If Snail pitched, Pat would play left field, and our buddy, Tony, would get to play second base. Emmett seemed to confirm this when he walked over to Tony and said something, and then Tony got up and trotted out to second base. It seemed the new pitcher, a ringer the Van Lear team had hoped would be there from somewhere in West Virginia, hadn't shown up. With Snail pitching, Tony got his big break and would play second base. This was great! Although he had gotten into a game at Auxier and one at Prestonsburg, we had never seen Tony play with the town team. Finally, we were going to get to see our buddy play for the big boys, and we had already started to speculate on how many hits he would get, and whether or not Snail Lambert, who was now taking his warmup pitches, could throw as hard as Paul Derringer of the Cincinnati Reds.

"He's got a better curve ball," I argued, although how I could know that from that one game in Cincinnati when we had sat halfway to Columbus, was anybody's guess. That had been a few years ago, however, and none of the others had been there, so I felt I had every right to make that judgment about Snail and Paul.

"Play ball!" the crowd yelled. The fans were growing restless and, pretty soon, the homeplate umpire walked up to a spot in front of the plate, removed his mask and held it in front of his chest protector. "Today's batteries," he announced in a loud voice directed first one way and then the other, "for the visiting Paintsville team, Chandler and Stout. For Van Lear, Lambert and Daniels. Play ball!"

The first three innings were scoreless. Snail mixed up his fast ball and curve just right, breaking the curve off where old Ab held his mitt. Ab yelled encouragement, standing upright and stabbing the air with the ball before returning it to our masterful moundsman. "Attaway, Snail," he cheered, "attaway to go. Bring it on in here, babe." The few Paintsville batters who managed to make contact with the ball sent grounders to third or short, and Tony handled his one and only chance flawlessly.

Chandler, the opposing Paintsville pitcher, who looked like an Indian, was equally skillful hurling the old horsehide. Pat McCoart hit the only ball out of the infield, but it was caught by the Paintsville centerfielder. Only Paul Butcher reached first, but that was on an error by their shortstop. It was definitely a pitchers' duel as the game went into the fourth inning. In the fourth, Junior Butcher connected for a homer, far up and over the right-centerfield fence, a good three hundred fifty feet or more. But Paintsville's little shortstop made up for his earlier error by tagging one over the rightfield fence in the sixth. The game was all tied at one run each, last of the ninth, with Danny Butcher, Pat McCoart, and Tony due to bat. What a spot for our buddy, Tony, to be in!

Chandler then set Danny Butcher down on three straight pitches, but Pat McCoart drew a walk, bringing up Tony. The Paintsville pitcher bore down on him, sensing that the man at the plate represented a potential double play. The big righthander took forever to get the sign. Then, he stretched and held Pat on base, making several throws to first in an attempt to catch the runner leaning toward second. In between throws to first, he glared at Tony. The big pitcher's countenance was so menacing I had the distinct feeling that he would like to tear Tony limb from limb. Finally, when he delivered the ball to the plate, it was wide and outside, but Tony, overeager, swung and missed by a country mile. "Tha's aw'right," someone yelled, "only takes one." Almost everyone was now cheering for Tony, but just then a terrible thing happened: Chandler repeated his agonizing routine and this time, on his third throw to first, he actually caught Pat off-balance and picked him off, clean as a whistle. Two down, last of the ninth, and it was now all up to Tony or the game would go into extra innings.

The Paintsville pitcher was really bearing down now. You could see that he sensed an easy third out. He wound up and threw. Bam! Strike two! He retrieved the ball and rubbed it up while walking off the mound. Back on the mound, he hitched up his pants, spit, and looked in for the sign. Confidently, he took a full windup and delivered a fast one high and inside, hitting Tony on his shoulder. Tony shrugged it off and loped down to first. This brought up Junior Butcher, who had accounted for our team's one and only run with his homer. Junior stood at the plate and glared at the pitcher who glared back. I could see their pitcher's lips move. "Big man, Junior Butcher!" he said, defiantly. While the two of them glared at each other, Tony, unnoticed, took off for second, slid in safe, and the crowd roared.

This shook up the Paintsville pitcher. He stretched, and looked long and hard at Tony, who was leading off second. He peeked in at the batter, then whirled and threw the ball toward his second baseman, who was supposed to slip in behind the runner. As all true baseball fans know, this was a foolish thing to do with two men out. The risk of error is always too great, and Tony was already on his way to third and running hard. Emmett Lambert, coaching at third, waved him on. The ball bounded over an uncovered second base into centerfield, but the Paintsville centerfielder, who had anticipated the pick-off play, retrieved the ball almost immediately and pegged it home.

The ball and Tony arrived at homeplate almost in a dead heat.

When the dust cleared, the umpire stood over them, his legs wide apart. For an instant, he hesitated. Tony had slid through the legs of the catcher, who had made a swipe at him and was still holding the ball. It was a close one, no doubt about it. Cries of "Safe! He's Safe!" went up throughout the park. Finally, almost in heart-stopping, agonizing slow-motion, the ump confirmed what all the home fans were rooting for when he flattened out the palms of both of his hands, spread his arms wide and yelled, "Safe!"

It was one of the sweetest wins ever. Nothing like it would happen, maybe ever again in our entire lives. Only our football and basketball games against the Paintsville High School Tigers later that year would come anywhere near equaling that triumph, and no other game could compare with it for sheer gut-wrenching drama. Nothing could ever erase it from our memories. It would go down in the annals of Van Lear athletics as The Day Tony Stole Home.

As we walked back to our homes that day, Richard, Billy, and I dredged up from memory the details of that game and composed a poem, a take-off on "Casey at the Bat":

> *The contest went the limit*
> *between the two opposing nine.*
> *The score was tied at one to one;*
> *the game was on the line.*
>
> *Oh, somewhere in this favored land,*
> *the sun is shining bright,*
> *the fireworks now are bursting forth*
> *and lighting up the night.*
>
> *And that somewhere's a mining town*
> *where mighty Bankmules play;*
> *where they celebrate their victory;*
> *where hearts are light and gay.*
>
> *But there is no joy in Paintsville town;*
> *no one is laughing there;*
> *for our second baseman Tony*
> *has beat them fair and square.*

We knew that our poem wasn't very original, but we liked it and the next week we decided that we would print it in our kid newspaper. Even Walter and Bill pitched in, and because the event was so special, we decided to call that issue the *Van Lear Gazette-Dispatch*. It sold out right away with a circulation of at least ten copies.

One day following the big game I looked down the road and saw a car stop. My dog Lucky raced over to the car and the men in it let old friendly Lucky jump right in, and they then sped off, and that was the last I saw of Lucky for almost a full year. That dog was really special to me. Aunt Bryda, Mom's sister, had given him to me one day in Ashland when she said her daughter Lyda was now grown and no longer needed a pet. I stood there looking down the road, wondering what I might do to get my dog back.

This photo was made in 1985, some fifty years after Hondel Adams (VLHS 1943) and I played hooky and rode over to Daniels Creek to find my dog Lucky. Here, Hondel, then a pastor of a Macedonian Christian Church, examines a copy of Blue Moon, *while I sign one of the books, and Bill Petry and Dallas Pinkerton look on.*

Soon we were high school sophomores, and I had heard nary a word about my dog. Hondel Adams met me one morning and told me that he thought we might find him over on Daniels Creek. The next day, the two of us played hooky, rode our bikes up to Number 5, and then pushed them to the top of the hill, and coasted down the dirt road to Daniels Creek. We had gone scarcely a mile down the hill, when Hondel pointed to a wire fence and a gate at the mouth of one of the smaller hollers. Sure enough, there was old Lucky, yapping like a mad dog. When we went over to him, he acted like he would tear us apart. He didn't even know who I was. We tried to tame him, but nothing seemed to work. Finally, we left. That was the last time that I would see my old pal Lucky.

That fall, my brother noticed that my feet had outgrown his old shoes, and he told me that I should go to the store and tell Erwin Brown that he sent me there for a new pair of shoes. I could still wear George's hand-me-down clothes but not his shoes, and I was glad to get that new pair of oxfords. When I brought those new shoes home, I carefully put them away, and wore them only on special occa-

Bobby Lambert guards Richard Sparks on the concrete surface that we uncovered in 1940 where the old mule barn once stood. It was here that we played off-season basketball, hoping to become as proficient at that game as the boys from Inez.

sions. Ordinarily we still went shoeless or else wore our old tennis shoes, which were our chosen footwear now that basketball had become a consuming passion.

I think it was our desire to try to reach the level of the Inez boys in basketball that prompted Richard and me to practice on our own, but we had no level place to play. One day, Mister Sparks suggested that we could scrape off a place where the old mule barn once stood, and use that as a practice court. Once we found and uncovered the old concrete floor, we coaxed a used telephone pole out of the carpentry shop foreman, and Richard's dad gave us an old truck wheel. We hammered the spokes out of the wheel, mounted it to a wooden backboard, and attached this to the pole. Eureka! We had our basketball goal, sans net, and a level, concrete surface on which to play. When our coach saw what we were doing he gave us an old basketball, and Richard and I spent the rest of that summer shooting baskets, one-on-one.

For nighttime entertainment we Van Lear boys preferred movies over radio programs, but movies cost money and a dime wasn't always to be had. Even though we were getting older and growing up and now had money of our own, which we earned from part-time jobs, we knew that our mothers were still in charge, and they frowned on our going anywhere other than church on Wednesdays, which was prayer-meeting night, and on Sundays to church and Sunday school. While we respected our mothers' wishes and did as we were told most of the time, we went to movies any other night we could scrape up the price of admission. We had lots of movie star idols. Bela Lugosi was a favorite vampire-type actor, and we went through the cowboy phase when practically every movie we saw was a western, and each of us assumed the role of a real-life cowboy actor. My favorite cowboy was Tim McCoy, whom I met many years later. I learned that my cousin, Alberta Vaughan, had been his leading lady in one of his movies, *Daring Danger*. The movies taught us lots of things, like how to smoke cigarettes, although I didn't take up that habit until much later in life, and the

This is a good picture of the old Rec building as it appeared shortly after the Company built a fence and added landscaping around it. Hollyhocks were planted in the center, with Lombardy poplars at the edge of the parking lot.

movies also taught us how to be snobs about things like the kind of music we listened to.

Richard and I hadn't cared much for *It Happened One Night* even though it won most of the Oscars the year it came out. But we had started to hum songs like "Blue Moon," Cole Porter's "I Get a Kick out of You," and songs from other movies. When Walter overheard Richard and me singing "I Get A Kick Out Of You," he pointed out to us that the lyrics referred to the use of cocaine. It didn't mean much to Richard and me at the time, just to Walter, who had decided he would try for a career in medicine, and so he was reading anything and everything of a scientific nature that he could find. Richard and I, on the other hand, were both inclining at this particular time toward what we regarded as more glamorous work, like newspaper reporting and radio broadcasting. Our interest in newspapers was acquired in a variety of ways, one of which was the Louisville *Courier-Journal*, which offered free trips to carrier boys who could sell twelve new subscriptions. The summer between my sophomore and junior year, Richard, Hondel, John, Humpy, Leo, Teamus , Dick and I managed to sell a total of 96 paper subscriptions which was enough to earn a trip to Louisville for all eight of us.

For the newspaper trip, we were transported in Greyhound buses rather than rail coaches, which we would have preferred. On the first night, we were deposited on one floor of the Lafayette Hotel in Lexington, five or six boys to a room. Then we were taken on a trip through the Bluegrass and a visit to Keeneland and Calumet Farm, a real eye opener for us kids from the hills. The following day, we went on to Louisville, where we were joined by carrier boys from around the state.

The first thing on our agenda in Derby Town was a tour of the newspaper plant, and this was a most impressive thing to see, especially the casting of the curved metal plates used to print the paper. After the tour of the newspaper plant, we were free to return to our hotel, which was directly across the street from the National Theater. After traipsing about the downtown area for an hour or two, most of us went like lemmings, to the old National, where the principal attraction was a slightly naughty vaudeville show. On the ornate stage, during the finale, we were treated to a sight that every male yearns to see in his young life. There, in real-life living color, we boys from Van Lear saw our first female nude. We were mightily impressed with this vision of beauty. Not only was that nude figure full and lithesome with just the right curvature, her face was pretty and unworldly as well. This maiden's body—and each of us saw her as pure as the driven snow—was even more erotic because she stood there, motionless as a statue, glistening provocatively from head to toe in luminescent golden body paint. She was our Golden Girl, a title we unanimously bestowed upon her right then and there. As I search for a way to describe my condition, I can only tell you that I was visibly aroused, and I'm pretty certain that the other guys were too. Word about the luscious nude spread like wildfire amongst the Kentucky newspaper carriers, and every kid on that newspaper trip must have been there that evening at the late show. Richard and I had a hard time finding a good seat down front, and we got there early.

The following day, with the memory of the previous day's events still fresh in our minds, we boarded street cars and made our way west to the old fairgrounds and the Kentucky State Fair. The street cars were coupled together, three to a set, forming a kind of train. Some of the younger boys jumped up and down and screamed like stuck pigs, and the tour guides from the newspaper tried to corral and contain them. This sort of embarrassed us Van Lear boys. We decided that this kind of behavior was beneath us, and so we remained seated, with smugly superior looks on our faces, trying hard to act like sophisticates from right there in Louisville, instead of hicks from the hills.

When we arrived at the fair, we cast aside our sophistication and reverted to just being boys. With our curiosity whetted, one of our first visits was to the sideshow that featured a hermaphrodite—"morphidite" in our native tongue—that single person cursed with organs of both sexes. Few us found this even mildly arousing, and when we heard the barker advertising the girlie show, none of us paid the extra two bits. After the previous night's vision of beauty, these maidens weren't even in the running. We finished the day with a cruise aboard a steamboat on the Ohio River.

With nothing more to do that summer, Richard Adams and his cousin Hondel and I decided that we would enroll in some vocational courses at the Mayo Vocational School in Paintsville, which had been established a year or two earlier, thanks in part to our state representative, a Van Lear miner named John Mollette, who had sued the state mine inspector the year my dad and the other miners lost their lives in the explosion. The way the school was established makes for a colorful story all by itself. It seems that one of Representative Mollette's colleagues from downstate took exception to the plan to establish the Mayo school, since he felt it would take money away from his district. An argument ensued, and Mollette fired his pistol into the air, right inside the capitol building, rending a hole in the dome, which is said to exist to this day.

Once we decided on our latest venture, we rode our bicycles to the school for the next five weeks, and learned something about electricity and house-wiring, and drafting and blue-print reading. What prompted us to undertake this extracurricular learning is something that I cannot explain. The electricity part included wiring a house, which is something that I was able to do without assistance many years later when I built my own home.

Regular school was, for our gang, a mixed experience. For some, it was a kind of penalty they paid for having fathers who worked for a company that wouldn't tolerate truancy. For Richard and me, it was something we managed quite well. Although I was a year ahead of Richard, in age and in school, we were friendly competitors, academically and athletically. By the time I found myself in the eleventh grade, however, athletics and social activities had put my interest in book learning on a back burner, so to speak. I still made good grades, but they weren't always A's. Toward the end of our first semester that year, Mister Lewis called me aside to tell me that I would most likely receive a B in his English class, since I had failed to do some required work, and he asked me if I would like to take on an additional project to bring that grade back up to an A-level. He explained that I could do a term paper on a topic of my own choosing, perhaps something on the order of "Building a Coast-to-Coast Military Highway Across The United States." I don't know how he happened upon that idea, but it appealed to me immediately, and he said I could think about it over the weekend, which I did. As I pondered, I could envision such an engineering miracle, a big divided highway, with two lanes running in each direction, with limited but easy access, and—most important, I thought—that highway would by-pass towns and cities, and would be an "express" highway. When confronted with the need to answer Mister Lewis, I declined his offer and accepted a B for the half-year's work in English. Basketball and other matters were receiving more and more of my time and attention.

I shot this picture of our old Van Lear High School building around 1948, but it looked much the same during our student days there, from 1939 through 1943. It was in Mister Lewis' second-floor eleventh-grade English classroom that I was challenged to raise my grade from "B" to "A."

Throughout the autumn of 1941, my mother tuned her radio to H.V. Kaltenborn and Lowell Thomas, who kept her informed on what was going on in the world. What was going on was war in Europe, and although the United States was not yet in it, Mom seemed to sense that it was only a matter of time until that too would change. "The Nazis have taken Poland," Thomas announced one day in that wonderful voice of his. "Who will be next? France? Belgium?"

Shortly afterwards, I overheard my mother telling our neighbor Pearl O'Bryan, "James Elwood may have to go off to war before long." When I heard her say that, I understood why she had let me go on that trip to Louisville. No one who lived in Van Lear or in Johnson County had all that much money, except for the mine managers and, I guess, a few merchants. However, most coal-miner parents indulged their sons, in part at least because the world seemed to be falling down all around them, and their boys might not live beyond the war, already underway in Europe. The country still hadn't recovered from the Great Depression, yet Mom and my brother—George was now in the Army Signal Corps—had been able to keep our little family together. Food was cheap—a gallon of milk was twenty cents and a loaf of bread eight cents—and most of the things we did for fun were free. During my junior year, our lives centered around varsity athletics, something that had always diverted us from the cares of our everyday world.

You already know about our prowess on the baseball diamond. Now, I must tell you, the Van Lear Bankmules also had a fearsome reputation on the gridiron. It all dated back to the early days when the mine superintendent brought Eddie Congleton to town to teach in the high school. Eddie had played some collegiate football, so he picked up where Coach Welch had left off, and taught the local boys what he knew about football. The word went out that families with big, strapping boys would be welcomed additions in Van Lear. They came from all over, north and south, and the Van Lear Bankmules were soon running roughshod, as the sportswriters of the day might say, over many of their high school opponents in the valley. During the 1920s and 1930s, they seldom had a losing season.

The sport, as taught by Coaches Congleton, Holland, Venari, Ison, Chambers, and Branham, was both rough and, at the same time, gentlemanly. The winning team would always gather in a huddle and give fifteen cheers for the losing team, and the losers would return the favor. The two principal rivalries that stand out were the matchups between Van Lear's Bankmules, and Jenkins' Cavaliers, another Consolidation Coal Company town, and—perhaps even more bitterly contested—the perennial battle between Van Lear and Paintsville. Despite the loss of some really good athletes like Gene Auxier, Elmer Price, Homer Cunningham, Bill Burchwell, and Art McCoart in 1928, the two schools fought the following year on mostly

One of the early Van Lear Bankmule football teams. Coach Eddie Congleton, in the white sweatshirt, also taught violin. He received his Ph.D. in 1936 from the University of North Carolina and, after teaching in Turin, Italy, he spent twenty-two years as a professor of English at the University of Florida.

even terms until the final whistle, when Bill Layne and Hut Robinson pulled out a last-minute touchdown to overcome the valiant efforts of Otchel Daniels, Virgil Porter, and their Bankmule teammates. About the Van Lear athletes, Coach Jesse Holland later remarked, "Those boys could have beaten any team if they used their heads, but they would rather run over an opponent instead of running around him." One of the last football victories Van Lear enjoyed over the county seat rival occurred in 1935 when Howard Kazee, known locally as Peanut, ran back the opening kickoff one hundred yards for a touchdown.

The sport of football had been put on hold in 1939, and the 1940 football season would witness the last exhibitions on the gridiron by a team representing Van Lear High School. Coach Estill "Eck" Branham had some outstanding talent, but, as always, the squad lacked depth. Denver Wells, Tony Clifton, Chi Chi Campigotto, and Clyde Groves were the four backs, with reserves Clifford Honaker, Bobby Lambert, Clyde Collins, Vencil Young, and Russell Rice. On the line were Jimmy Ward, Brownlo Wells, Jr., Frankie Cunningham, Alex Pelphrey, Herschel Blair, Arnold Dixon, and Sebert Wells, with Oral Trimble, Hondel Adams, Ty Wallace, Jimmy Hall, Bob Daniels, Earl Dixon, and Marion Castle in reserve, a squad so lean in numbers it was necessary to call on the help of former players to have an intrasquad scrimmage. An abortive attempt was made by Dick Stapleton to continue football the following year, but from then on, the emphasis was on basketball.

With football season behind us, we were free to enjoy the fall weather and scenery, even the gray, rainy days, which sometimes turned cold and bleak overnight, but the cold weather had its good side, like coal fires in the fireplaces, big navy blue school sweaters with the bold letter V in gray on the front, long walks in the leaf-strewn woods, sorghum-making, Halloween, and time to reflect on and brag about all we had done during another eventful, and often fun-filled year in Van Lear.

As the final leaves of autumn turned and tumbled from the trees and the wind grew brisk, our thoughts and energies were once more directed to basketball, although it was rarely the strongest suit in the Bankmules' athletic deck. Quite often some smaller school would not only win the district and regional tournaments, but would go on to show the big schools from down-state a thing or two about that sport. Those smaller schools couldn't muster enough young stalwarts to man a football team, but they were usually able to find five eagle-eyed boys from up in the hollers, who could thread a needle with a roundball. Teams from these smaller schools practiced year-round under the watchful eye of a dedicated coach who devoted himself to that task and little else. Meade Memorial, across the ridges near Greasy Creek, and Inez in Martin County were two such schools, and both of them were in our district, along with Louisa and Paintsville.

During the 1940 - 41 basketball season, some basketball fans, and even a few sports writers, thought that Van Lear or Paintsville might at least have a shot at the district title, but there would be both Meade and Inez to reckon with, both teams with deadeyed shooters like Meade's Paul Butcher. In fact, the Inez coach Russell Williamson had five deadeyes, in Charles Kirk and Lester West at the guards, Bob Cooper at center, and Bill Taylor at one forward position, opposite little sharpshooter Alex Harmon.

Van Lear's squad that year included Richard Sparks, Oral Trimble, Clyde Groves, Tony Clifton, Clifford Honaker, Russell Rice, Hondel Adams, Marcus Spears, Buddy Meade, and me. I jumped center. Our Coach Eck Branham, who had played varsity sports at Western Kentucky, really thought we had a good chance to win our district, even though we were up against at least three other good teams in Meade, Inez, and Paintsville. After a so-so season of 16 wins, and 12 losses, we hosted the District Sixteen tournament in

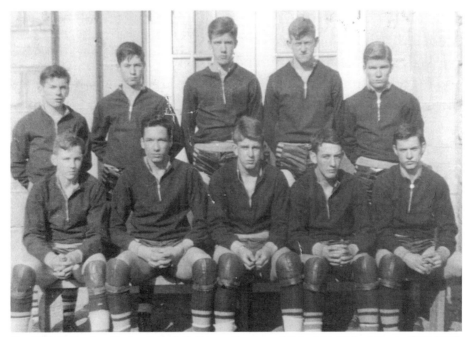

Our 1940-41 Van Lear Bankmule Basketball team. Front row, left to right, Richard Sparks (PHS 1944), James Vaughan (AHS 1943), Clyde Groves (VLHS 1942), Clifford Honaker (PHS 1942), and Tony Clifton (VLHS 1943). Second row, Hondel Adams (VLHS 1943), Russell Rice (VLHS 1942), Marcus Spears (VLHS 1943), Leonard Meade(VLHS 1943), and Oral Trimble (VLHS 1942). Members of this team met defeat in a district tournament game against Russell Williamson's Inez Indians, who went on to win the overall Kentucky State Basketball Championship over Saint Xavier of Louisville. Inez players Charles Kirk, Lester West, Bob Cooper, Bob Taylor, and Alex Harmon later served in our country's armed forces during World War II, as did all of the members of this Van Lear team.

our WPA-built limestone gymnasium at Van Lear. Feeling fairly confident, we managed to make quick work of the team from Louisa in our opening round game. But then we drew Inez, and I came down with the flu. Bob Cooper towered over almost any center he faced, and he was a good twelve inches taller than Russell Rice, who Coach Branham inserted in my stead. The game wasn't close. In the district tournament final, Meade Memorial managed to eke out a close win over Inez, thanks to good rebounding from their center, a big bruiser named Cam, and some sharp shooting by Paul Butcher. Both teams then continued to the regional tournament, which Inez won handily. Coach Branham took us down to Lexington, and we watched Coach Williamson's Inez boys win the overall Kentucky State Basketball Championship, disposing of St. Xavier of Louisville in the finals.

Van Lear's starting five in the fall of 1941 were Richard Sparks and Oral Trimble at the guard positions, Buddy Meade at one forward and Tony Clifton at the other, and at six-foot-two, I jumped center. Shortly after the season got underway, Denver Wells came back from the army, older and wiser, and he and Oral alternated at one guard position. In reserve, the Bankmules had Sebert Wells, Jimmy Hall, Jack Williams, and Russell Rice.

Once again, a number of sports writers thought that the 1941-42 season could be different, that our team might have a shot at the district title, but this time both Paintsville and Inez would be contenders. Vernon Honeycutt had been enticed to leave his Auxier squad, which included two outstanding players in Red Bickford and Bugdust Evans, to come to Van Lear to coach us. Under Coach Honeycutt, we had a somewhat better season, splitting games with our county-seat rival, the Paintsville Tigers. We won our home-floor game against Paintsville with a slow-down, freeze-the-ball kind of offense. This was before the shot clock, and five-second rule. You could literally "hold" the ball, without advancing it, ever, and the rules also allowed teams to elect to shoot one free throw, and take the ball out of bounds in lieu of a second shot. The free throw lane was also narrow, giving real meaning to the expression, "keyhole," and I was able to play the post in the key and take advantage of that inside position in many of our games. In our low-scoring game against Paintsville, we won by a margin of 19 to 10, and I had nine points. My best game was against Blaine when I had 23 points. For the season I averaged around 16 points, thanks to a turn-around jump shot that Coach Honeycutt taught me.

Midway through the season, everything was changed with the news, on the seventh day of December, that the Japanese had bombed Pearl Harbor. I recall that Sunday quite vividly. We were at home reading the Sunday paper, following church service, when Mitchell Adams came down the road from the Fountain. He had heard the latest bulletin uptown. Mom and I went inside and tuned our radio to WLW and listened intently. Her prediction was coming true, but not in the way she had envisioned it. The following day, I listened to President Roosevelt's momentous speech to a joint session of Congress: "Yesterday, December 7th, 1941, a day that will live in infamy…"

It was March of 1942, the first round in the big district tournament, and all bets were off on that game. As luck would have it, we drew Inez in the opening round. Although Coach Williamson had lost most of his starting five from his state championship team of 1941, he had brought along an equally well-coached team, including clever red-headed twin guards, and a big center named Curtis Ward. Nicknamed "Big Stoop," Curtis stood six feet, six inches, towering over almost every other center he was matched against. I would jump center with him.

Inez got the opening tip, but Oral caused a turnover and brought the ball downcourt. If we couldn't fast-break, we always tried to set it up, and run patterns. Whenever we got a shot off, our coach expected our goal to be surrounded by four Van Lear Bankmules, each ready to rebound, and the point guard—Oral, in this case—always back-pedaled to the opponent's end of the floor on defense in case the other team got the ball. All of the Bankmules were good shooters, and the scoring was usually evenly distributed. Sometimes I had a good game with my one-handed turn-around jump shot and tip-ins. At other times, it might be Buddy with his patented two-handed jump shot from the side, or Richard, Tony, Denver, or Oral, and their set shots. Sebert, Jimmy, Russell, and Jack always could be depended on to provide good rebounding.

Our Van Lear Bankmule Cheerleaders in 1941: Eloise Hall, Naomi Rucker, and Virginia Meddings (all VLHS 1942).

Our first offensive effort failed to shake anyone loose. The Indians were playing a tight zone. Next time around, Richard signaled to bring me out to the side just a bit, opening up the middle so that we could have a little more room to maneuver should someone get the ball at the top of the circle. We then began zinging the ball around the Indian's perimeter defense, hoping, through speedy ball-handling, to edge closer and closer in toward the goal until, finally, someone would have a reasonably open and uncontested shot at the basket. Very little, if any dribbling of the ball, just zip, zip, zip.

In those days, high school basketball players in our part of the world were all white, and mostly slow and heavy-legged. The teams were more disciplined, partly due to the coaching of people like Baron Adolph Rupp at the University of Kentucky, Henry Iba out in Oklahoma, and Ed Diddle at Western Kentucky. Richard had sunk a two-handed shot, but it had been from twenty feet, and this didn't exactly please Coach Honeycutt, who now sat glaring across court, motioning the Van Lear five to hurry back down court on defense. He too was a devotee of the slow, deliberate and conservative style of Rupp and Iba. He wanted his teams to shoot from close-in, like five feet away from the basket. One of the twin guards sank a two-hander for Inez, and we Bankmules knew that we were in for a tough

Some of the individuals involved in our 1942 tournament game are pictured in these three photos, which were shot forty-three years later. At the top are Iris Ward Blair (VLHS 1944), me, Dorothy Pack Meade (VLHS 1946), and Leonard "Buddy" Meade (VLHS 1943). In the middle are Arnold Blanton and Worth Goble (both VLHS 1943). Below are, left to right, me, Verne Horne, Clyde Phelps (VLHS 1943), Russell Rice (VLHS 1942), and Buddy Meade.

time of it as we struggled back and forth for the first six minutes with neither team gaining an advantage. Finally, Coach called time.

Arnold Blanton, the team manager, handed a couple of towels to us as we gathered around to listen to Coach Honeycutt's counsel. "No more zone," he told us. "Their guards're shootin' over us. Go to our old shifting man-to-man defense. Stay in their faces and be sure to check off. Talk to each other. 'Kay?" We nodded and went back to the fray. "And don't let your man run over a screen," he yelled.

When we went into the dressing room at halftime, the score was all tied at nineteen points each. During the mid-game break, Coach Honeycutt told us, if we fell behind or if the score was still close going into the last four minutes, he would motion us to start a full-court press on defense, and we knew all too well what that meant. We would be in constant motion, and we had better be in good physical shape. Offensively, he told us that we must keep the ball moving as long as Inez stayed in a zone, and we should only take the good wide-open shot. There wasn't much more that could be said. We Bankmules knew what we had to do. If we got the lead, we were to freeze the ball with a four-corners set-up.

It went right down to the wire, down to the last twenty seconds, tied at 29 - 29. The Inez guard, who opened their scoring, brought the ball downcourt, passed off to the other Indian guard, who gave it right back to his mate, and that little guard let fly with another two-hander, but it was wide of the mark. I rebounded the ball and handed it off to Richard. Oral Trimble went straight for the hoop, and we thought he was fouled, but there was no call. The noise in the gym was so loud we couldn't hear ourselves think. Then, with only seconds remaining on the clock, Big Stoop drew a nonshooting foul, and the big guy walked calmly to the foul line and sank the free throw, and that's how Van Lear lost its first game in the district tournament that year.

After the game, my brother told me that Ellis Johnson wanted to talk to me. Ellis, who had officiated our game, was head basketball coach at Morehead State College. He had played both football and basketball at Ashland and, later, at UK, where he achieved All-America status in both sports. During our brief encounter he told me that I should come down to see him after graduation, and he could offer me an athletic scholarship.

There were several more memorable moments in our youthful lives that stand out, each etched forever in our memories. One in particular occurred on a cold, snowy day in February. Oral Trimble, who

Van Lear cheerleader Virginia Meddings appears to be holding me aloft one wintry day in 1941.

had dropped out of school to join the Navy, had been in the service less than two months. After a short boot camp, he was assigned to a destroyer in the Atlantic. Word of his death came on a Sunday, a day when a few of our Van Lear gang had planned a special outing. Oral's destroyer had been on submarine patrol as an escort vessel for a Lend Lease convoy to Great Britain, and a German sub had spotted her and sent her to the bottom of the Atlantic with a single torpedo. The whole crew was lost. My cousin Charles Vaughan had met a similar fate a year earlier.

Four of us had planned a sleigh ride outing. At first, we considered canceling it, but then we thought better of it. It turned out to be

Oral Trimble, 1942, a year before he lost his life in the navy.

a delightful day. There was no other way to describe it. There were only the four of us: Billy, Bobby, Richard, and me. We bundled up in our winter garb, and went out into the bracing air. Richard's dad provided one of his trucks onto which we loaded two homemade bob-sleds. Richard drove the truck, and I sat in the cab with him. Billy and Bobby climbed aboard, and we went charging off, the powdery snow crunch-ing beneath the vehicle's treads, bouncing along all the way to the football field. There, at the entrance to Garland Webb's farm, we turned off and drove across the creek and up behind the Webb home, where the hillside and swale there made a natural amphitheater and one of the world's best bobsled runs.

We had great fun that evening. Soon, several others joined us. We built two big bonfires, one at the top and one at the bottom of the slope, and there was the thrill of the rides, two to the sled, hang-ing onto each other and screaming at the tops of our lungs; and there were the long, joyful walks back up to the top, talking and reveling in each other's company, wishing the day would never end. Idyllic, a word rarely used today, a word we had learned in junior high school under Miss Wheatley, best described that day. Some-how, despite that great afternoon, all of us sensed that things were changing and would never be the same again. The sudden loss of Oral had heightened our awareness of what might lie ahead. If Andrew Lloyd Webber had been around then and had written that haunting melody from *Cats*, the one titled "Memory," it would have filled our minds and hearts on many a poignant and bittersweet occasion that year and in years to follow, striking just the right chord to complement our melancholy mood. I think we all knew that we might never again have this kind of fun.

My brother George was now in training in the Army, soon to be shipped with his Signal Corps unit to Great Britain, where they would await the D-Day invasion of Europe. Large numbers of young Van Lear men enlisted in various branches of the service. For me, the worst was yet to come. My mother was now considering marriage to Joe Williamson, Consol's carpentry and maintenance supervisor, and Lacey's father. He had also lost a spouse. But my mother's plans were soon changed. Mom had breast surgery, and the growth they removed was malignant. She was now making regular trips to Ashland for x-ray and radium therapy, and the prognosis was not good. It would be much easier on Mom if we moved to Ashland where she could be nearer her doctors. As soon as my junior year in high school ended, we packed up and moved, taking rented rooms on the second floor of the house owned by my mother's sister Aunt Minnie Lyons, across from Central Park.

Before I departed, I went alone one day to the hill overlooking the old football field, and sat down on a log in a sea of brown leaves, and thought about all the good times and bad times from our growing-up days in Van Lear. As I sat there all alone in the stillness of the early evening, the haunting whistle of a passenger train echoed across the creek, down the railroad, and through the hills, and I thought of that long-ago day when Dad had taken me on that memorable excursion to Cincinnati; and then I remembered other days, and I could almost hear our school fight song, and the cadences that had been sung to celebrate victories and mourn defeats. When my thoughts turned to the sadder things, it was as though I was in a kind of Bankmules' Valhalla, a final gathering place for those who had fought there, both above and beneath the ground on which I sat, and I was having some second thoughts about some things. Although Van Lear had been a good place for a boy like me to grow up, I had begun to wonder if it had really been as neat as I had always made it out to be. We hadn't had all the money in the world, or all the toys and gadgets and stuff, and I remembered the death of my father, and the others, burned and crushed to death under piles of rock and slate, but then I recalled the other run-down coal camps and the hungry kids I had seen, and I decided, yes! Our town had been special!

As I sat there gazing out at an Appalachian autumn and its fading splendor, and wondering about the whereabouts of my buddies who had gone into the military services, I thought about the good times, the friendly and helpful people, and the never-changing world in which we had lived, and then, quite suddenly, I had this strange feeling that, after the war, our unchanging world wouldn't be the same, not for me or Richard or anybody and most especially for tomorrow's youth. In this almost apocalyptic moment, I had a vision of a new world in which the only predictable thing would be constant change, a world in which youthful imaginations like ours would no longer be allowed to flourish as had ours. Instead of the friendly people we once knew, instead of our Appalachian patriarchs and matriarchs, people who had had subtle influences on all of us, people who had been important sources of whatever character and wisdom we possessed, there would be greedy technocrats who would fill everyone's lives with chrome and plastic and things like television and other gadgetry, and there would be a lot of hypocritical posturing and mouthing by politicians and sociocrats about making things better for mankind, but it would all be a lie. Although I had never been particularly religious in any conventional way, I couldn't escape the feeling that our code of moral conduct would change, and we would no longer be the mostly moral people we once were, and everyone would be poorer for it.

I sat there stunned by these thoughts, unable to fathom where they came from or why they had occurred to me. It was rare for me to think things like this, much less have thoughts like this revealed to me in this manner.

That summer in Ashland I began working at Myron Bates' A&P store for thirty cents an hour, but I soon landed another job which paid sixty cents with Paul Blazer's Ashland Oil & Refining Company, working with a crew of grown men, tearing down the Tri-State Refinery at Ceredo-Kenova. Located adjacent to Dreamland,

This U.S.D.A. aerial photo shows the confluence of the Ohio and Big Sandy Rivers at Catlettsburg KY and Kenova WV with Dreamland and the Tri-State Plant visible above and left of the auto bridge.

An aerial view of South Point, Ohio, the Ohio River, Catlettsburg, Kentucky and Kenova, West Virginia. Paul Blazer's Tri-State plant was at the lower left at Virginia Point, just north and west of the highway bridge across the smaller Big Sandy River. The town of Kenova takes its name from its location where the three states meet.

a popular spot for Ashland and Huntington youth, a place which boasted a swimming pool and dance pavilion, the refinery was one of the first that Blazer bought when he started his oil business. It had outlived its usefulness, and it was our task to level it and make room for new storage tanks. In order to get the job, which doubled my pay, I had to join a union, the Oil Workers of America, my first and only such affiliation. Every day on my way to work, as we passed Dreamland, I looked out at the pool and wished that I could spend the day swimming there, rather than doing the dirty work assigned to us.

One of the members of our work crew was a man named Buck, who was the basketball coach at Grayson High School, which Ashland was scheduled to play in the fall, and I was pretty sure that I would be a member of the Ashland team. Another co-worker, the youngest other than me, was Charlie Snyder, who had just recently completed his high school career at Catlettsburg, where he had been an all-star football player. He would enter Marshall College in the fall. The other men were all married, drawing the same sixty cents an hour that I earned and supporting families on their pay.

The work was rough and dirty, to say the least, but no more so than coal mining, and certainly less dangerous. While one man cut steel with his acetylene torch, foreman Reeves had the rest of us dislodging bricks and hauling them in wheelbarrows, and loading them onto dump trucks. Still others stacked steel. One day we were sent out some distance from the refinery to find a gas leak. I was one of the workers chosen to get down in the pit with a shovel to dig and hunt for the leak. Before we found it, noxious fumes started oozing up out of the ground, and I began to get sick. Fortunately, the foreman saw what was happening and had someone take my place in the pit. At that time Ashland Oil was so small an organization, Paul Blazer himself sometimes came by to observe our work.

Cousin Harry Howell and his wife Wynne drove down from Flint, Michigan with his mother, my Aunt Mayme, and his father Uncle Bill Howell, who was quite ill with silicosis and emphysema. He had worked in the coal mines of southern Indiana, and his breathing had become difficult and labored. Aunt Minnie's husband Crocket Lyons, once a robust young foreman at the Norton Iron Works, had suffered a stroke after his marriage. After his disabling stroke, which paralyzed the left side of his body, Aunt Minnie, rented out rooms to provide for their livelihood. I recall that Uncle Bill and Uncle Crockett made a daily walk around Central Park. Those walks usually occupied the bulk of each morning, as neither Uncle Crockett nor Uncle Bill could manage much in the way of speed. I marveled at how these adults coped with misfortune, how they dismissed it as nothing out of the ordinary.

Wanda Lee Rice Vaughan, Bryda Lynk McGlothlin, and Minnie Lynk Lyons standing in front of Aunt Min's home on Central Avenue in Ashland, where I "boarded" in 1942, following the death of my mother. This photo was made in 1949.

Each evening I came home with brick dust and black oil all over my workclothes, which Aunt Min somehow managed to wash for me at the end of each workweek. During most of that long, hot summer, my mother lay abed, unable to continue the radiation treatments. Her left arm had become swollen and painful, and it was necessary for the doctor to visit her regularly to administer morphine and other pain-killing medicine. I tried to put this out of my mind as I went through my weekly work routine. Fortunately, Mom's sisters, Minnie and Mayme, were both there to minister to her personal needs.

One morning toward the end of July, Aunt Min met me at the front door as I started to leave to catch my ride to work. She told me that it would be better if I didn't go to work that day. She had called Mom's doctor, who soon arrived with his little black bag. I went upstairs with him and Aunt Min. He took one look at my mother, and reached into his bag. He placed some white tablets in a spoon and crushed them, and then he handed the spoon to me and told me to hold it. He added some sterile water, and then held a match under it, dissolving the crushed material into a clear liquid. I watched as he drew some of this into a syringe and injected into my mother's swollen arm.

My mother died later that day. Friends and neighbors came from Van Lear to attend her funeral services at the Pollard Baptist Church. The details of that week and the days that followed are pretty much a blur in my mind. Before that summer ended, Uncle Bill passed away. When Harry and his brothers came for the funeral, I recall how much I admired their manners and appearance. All of five them—Willard, Harry, Leonard, Raymond, and Chet—had good jobs with Buick, AC Sparkplug, or some other division of General Motors. We had visited them six years ago at their vacation cabins in northern Michigan, and I think it was then that I made up my mind that I wanted to be like them.

My senior year at Ashland Senior High School is something of an incomplete and indistinct memory, although certain events stand out in retrospect. The school was larger than what I had been accustomed to, of course. And, while we had been somewhat snobbish about country ways at Van Lear, I soon learned that many of my contemporaries at AHS were even more "citified." Soon after I enrolled, one of the sprightlier girls made a point of referring to me as "country," and I found that quaint. In all fairness, however, there were many who took me in as a friend and equal, including Jimmy Stinson, who had graduated a year earlier and who now had a car and a job with ARMCO. His mother and grandmother continued to operate a small grocery store after the death of his father, thus providing a family living in much the same way as my Aunt Minnie had taken hold as her family's breadwinner. Jimmy's cousin was Ty Wallace from West Van Lear, so we also had that in common. Actually, a good many of the people I knew in Ashland had ties "Up Big Sandy," but, for some reason or other, many of them were reluctant to admit it.

Football was bigger than basketball at Ashland, and Charley Ramey and Joe Rupert, the Ashland coaches, visited me soon after the school year began. They had taken over at AHS, knowing that they had the makings of a very good team, and they had heard from Aunt Min's neighbor Ernie Chattin that I was a likely prospect. In a way, I regret that I decided not to play that year, but I had developed a bad knee sprain that would plague me for the rest of my life. My decision was based on my belief that I could only manage one sport, and my best sport was probably basketball. The Ashland football Tomcats won all their games that fall, including a victory over Manual High of Louisville, and the overall Kentucky State Championship. Incidentally, I learned that Joe Rupert's dad George had been a conductor on the passenger train at Van Lear. Joe never mentioned his Big Sandy background to me. Another bit of trivia: Coach Ramey's red-headed sister Venus, then living in Washington D.C., was named Miss America the following year.

Charley Ramey also coached basketball. He was assisted by Ted Franz, who had basketball experience, but Coach Ramey made no pretensions about his lack of expertise in the roundball sport. I managed to make the team as its center, without undue pressure from anyone except Bill Elswick, and we had some pretty good talent in the likes of Bernard Pergram, Gerald Jarvis, and others, all younger and shorter than me, but we never developed into a real "team." The Van Lear Bankmules could have disposed of our Ashland Tomcats quite easily.

I recall that Ted Franz was surprised when he saw that I knew how to play basketball with a bit of style and grace, and he asked me who had coached me. My second-year algebra teacher Mrs. Roy

A Bankmule becomes a Tomcat. Here I am, jumping center against Raceland, 1942.

Smith was also taken aback when she realized that I had more than average ability in her subject. And, although most, if not all of the Ashland teachers were well-prepared, I felt that my Van Lear schooling had been superior in most respects. High School Principal James Anderson was less than pleased with me, particularly when I elected a non-college preparatory program, which included courses like auto mechanics and mechanical drawing, rather than more demanding subject matter.

We won our opening game against Raceland, although it was a close one, and the next week we boarded a Greyhound bus and went over to Grayson to play Coach Buck's boys. You will recall that Coach Buck had been one of my co-workers that summer, and I do believe that they were lying in wait for me and my Tomcat teammates. After another close game, they managed to put us away when we failed to develop any sort of consistent offense. I played in a few more games, and then decided that I wanted to start going out with girls on dates.

My mother had left me a small amount of money, which was held for me by my guardian, Case Layne, Cousin Ruby's husband, and while this enabled me to pay for room and two daily meals with Aunt Min, it left little or nothing for movies and such. When Ted Franz became aware of this, he sent me down to Sam Israel, owner of the Royal Jewelry Store on Winchester Avenue in down-

The year is 1942, and I am still wearing my letter sweater from VLHS, although now in my senior year at AHS. Cousin Case Layne, my newly appointed "guardian," is at the left, hugging our Cousin Ruth Helen Dixon. Behind her is my brother George, already in the Army Signal Corps. Over my left shoulder is Cousin Troy Dixon, soon to become a "Roger's Ranger." To his left are Cousins Jackie and Betty Dixon. In front of me are Cousins Ron Layne and Bob Dixon.

town Ashland. Mister Israel seemed to take a liking to me and hired me as his "go-for" and stock boy, paying me ten dollars a week. My schedule called for me to work after school, Monday through Friday, from four to six, and eight hours each Saturday. For these eighteen hours I received ten dollars, which figured out to be about fifty-five cents an hour. I don't know if I was worth it or not. My duties included cleaning the glass-topped show cases, carrying watches to and from Mister Ludorf, the watchmaker, sweeping and mopping the floors, cleaning the show windows, and doing anything else that Walter Wingo, the manager, directed me to do. Eventually, I was trusted to hand-carry each day's bank deposit to the Third National Bank. I also retrieved sets of china stored in the dusty attic, and washed them and got them ready for packing whenever a customer bought these items.

Mister Israel must have liked me and my work. Childless, he sponsored my membership in Key Club, and took me with him to Kiwanis meetings. Before the school year ended, he asked me what

Ashland Jeweler Sam Israel sponsored me in the Key Club, whose members are shown here at Ashland Senior High in 1942.

I planned to do, and he seemed somewhat shocked when I told him. Aunt Mayme's son Harry and his wife Wynne had sent word to Aunt Mayme that I should come to stay with them after I graduated from high school. I could, they said, start attending Michigan State while working at one of the GM plants in Lansing. Harry was then General Manager of the Oldsmobile forge plant.

"Why," Mister Israel asked, "would you want to do that?" He was genuinely surprised. "Stay here," he counseled me, "and you can manage my store some day."

I thanked him, but declined the offer. A couple of years later, his manager Walter Wingo departed and established his own jewelry and gift emporium at The Greenbriar in White Sulfur Springs, West Virginia.

During that final school year, I returned to Van Lear for visits on two occasions, and three of my buddies visited me in Ashland. Marcus Spears and Richard Adams came down for an overnight stay, and then Buddy Meade drove his dad's car down, and we double-dated. Jimmy Stinson was generous in sharing his car, and we used it on several occasions, including one trip to Greenup for a basketball tournament, where, I was told, I had handed my ticket to a man named Jesse Stuart. I was vaguely aware that he was a well-known author, but the only book title I could recall was his *Man with a Bull-tongue Plow*.

When graduation time arrived, I was at least in the top ten percent of my class, which surprised some. Aunt Mayme measured me for a new suit for graduation. Following presentation of our diplomas, I lost little time in saying my good-byes, and I then packed up and caught a train for Lansing, Michigan.

It should now be obvious to the reader that, while I lost my dear parents at a relatively young age, good fortune smiled on me by investing my young life with many good people, both family and friends. In Ashland, there were Aunt Min and Uncle Crockett Lyons, Aunt Mayme and Uncle Bill Howell, Cousins Case and Ruby Layne, Bill and Pauline Elkins, Uncle Everett and Aunt Maude Vaughan, Mom's sisters, Aunt Bryda and Aunt Kate, coaches Charley Ramey and Ted Franz, Sam Israel, Mister Ludorf, Walter Wingo, Cousins Frances and C.J. Bolton, the men I worked with at the Tri-State Plant, Myron Bates and the A&P Store, Jimmy Stinson, and Philip Lane, and then, following high school, Aunt Mayme's son Harry Howell and his dear wife Wynne. All of these people helped me along the way in one way or another, and to them I shall be eternally grateful.

Shortly after my arrival in Lansing, Wynne showed me to my room in their nice but unpretentious two-story home on Bartlett Street, and Harry took me down to Building 75 on the grounds of the Oldsmobile plant, where I signed on as a janitor. This was the only job I could qualify for under the then-current GM rules, as I was only seventeen years old. The plant produced armor-piercing three-inch shells for the navy on one line, and seventy-five millimeter shells for the army on a second line. The building had once housed an assembly line.

Manufacturing operations began with the delivery of ten-foot long round steel billets, each slightly more than three inches in diameter. These were loaded by cranes in bundles of three onto cradles which delivered them to electric saws that sawed them into ten-inch pieces. The second operation carried these pieces on conveyor lines to huge round machines called Bullards, where milling and boring operations trimmed the skin from the outer layer and drilled holes in the middle. Similar machines then honed the blunt end into an oval-shaped bullet nose, threaded the hole end, and ground out small dimples in the nose. After inspection of these projectiles for hidden flaws, armor-piercing caps were crimped into the dimples, streamlined nose cones were added and steel plugs inserted into the cavities. The finished product was shipped off to an ordnance plant where the projectiles would be loaded with explosives and attached to casings loaded with propellant. Paul Hutting and I, both being only seventeen, were not permitted to do this work officially, but we nevertheless operated every machine in the plant before the year was out, spelling the men when they wanted to "go to the can" for a smoke or otherwise. Our real job was to keep the place clean, and this involved constantly mopping up the milky cutting oil that was spilled out by the Bullard machines and removing the metal shavings for recycling. We tried to do this as quickly as possible, and then find someone who wanted to take a break for a smoke.

Meanwhile, I enrolled at Michigan State College, committing to courses in Freshman English, Foundry, and Mechanical Drawing, under the illusion that I had the makings of a mechanical engineer. My daily routine had me out of bed at seven, breakfasting with Harry at seven-thirty, riding a bus to East Lansing for my English class at eight, mechanical drawing at nine, foundry at ten, and then lunch. My work shift at the Olds plant was from three to eleven, followed by a walk home at midnight. Each workday, including Saturday, I repeated this routine, leaving Sunday as my only "free" day. Harry and Wynne loved to play golf. Harry gave me a set of his old clubs, and paid for my golf lessons by golf club pro, Olie Clark. Each Sunday, after dinner at the Walnut Hills Country Club, we played golf. When confronted with an opportunity to join the Michigan State College radio station as an apprentice announcer, I declined, little realizing that I would eventually end up working as a broadcaster.

Shortly after graduating from AHS in 1943, I journeyed to Lansing, Michigan, and took up residence with Cousins Harry and Wynne Howell. There I met this group of splendid fellows, including Paul Hutting, third from right at the rear, with whom I worked at the Oldsmobile plant. To his left is Paul Coulihan. It was Paul's father, a dentist and member of the naval reserve, who was largely responsible for my seeking admission to the Navy's V-5 pilot training program.

Among my new friends in Michigan, in addition to Paul Hutting, were Jim Spice and Paul Coulilhan, whose father was a dentist and a member of the Naval Reserve. In time, patriotism got the upper hand, and I longed to get into the fray. When Cousin Harry heard me talk about possibly trying for a spot in the Naval Aviation program, he offered to get me a tool and diemaker's apprenticeship, which would carry with it a deferment from the draft. He told me that I would have a different view of things when I grew older. But I had visions of flying off a carrier and shooting down Japs and that summer's routine was something I really didn't care for, even with a weekly golf outing. When I insisted on taking the V-5 exam, Harry had his friend Howard Couzens reserve a room for me at the Book Cadillac Hotel in Detroit.

The written tests were what you might call "rigorous," but I passed them and my physical without any problems. The flight aptitude test was a bit more difficult, particularly the depth perception part. Finally, the personal interview went well, but the photo I handed the interviewer was unsatisfactory, and so I stayed in Detroit another day, and sat for portrait at the J.L. Hudson Department Store. When I returned the following day, the interviewer was pleased with the result, and I went back to Lansing and awaited word. My acceptance came a month later, and I tendered my resignation, said my good-byes to Harry and Wynne, and reported to my assigned indoctrination point, Grosse Ile Naval Air Station on an island in Lake Erie, a short distance from Detroit.

My enlistment group, about seventy-five in number, came from all over Ohio and Michigan, with a like number from New York and New Jersey. We were assigned to duty on the air station as a company of Tarmacs, awaiting what we all hoped would be early assignments to preflight training. Grosse Ile had been assigned the task of providing primary training for Royal Air Force cadets, and our duties included servicing the Stearman biplanes used as their primary trainers. We were divided into two companies, one working a day shift and the other nights, with each company trading shifts every two weeks.

That winter was a cold one, with Lake Erie frozen over to a depth of two feet, and plowed snow stacked head-high along the roads from December through February. Our food was a menu prepared for the Limeys. Instead of coffee for breakfast, we were served hot tea with milk and sugar, and while we had scrambled eggs, they were the powdered variety. Instead of bacon, we often had kippers, which was a new experience for most of our crew. The young men who were there for primary training came from three sources, the British Royal Navy, the Royal Air Force, and the Royal Canadian Air Force. I got to know some of them, and they were a splendid lot, to say the least. Their country, of course, had been at war for three years, and had come dangerously close to defeat, early on. These young men received, on average, eight to ten hours of dual instruction, followed by a like number of hours in solo flight, including a few hours of night-flying, these latter flights with minimal ground lighting and, of course, few instruments. After this brief and rigorous regimen, they were sent back to England, where they soon found themselves in combat, flying Spitfires.

In early December, our commanding officer sent word to me and Mack Smith, who was from Seattle, that the station's basketball coach wanted to see us. It seems that he had seen the two of us play and was impressed, and so he had us work out with his team. They needed rebounding help, but could only use one more player. Somehow, they chose me over Mack, and I got to go on trips and play some in games against Bowling Green, Assumption College in Windsor, Ontario, and at Lincoln Park.

Our brief sojourn as Tarmacs was tolerable only because all of us anticipated flight training as Navy V-5 cadets. My brother George was in England where he and Uncle John's boys, Hubert and Johnny, and Everett's son, Warren, along with a number of my friends, were getting ready to be a part of the invasion of Hitler's Fortress Europe. This filled me with patriotic feelings and a desire to "get on" with our training. My fellow Tarmacs felt the same way. Finally, in early March, we were told that only three individuals from our Tarmacs would be selected for navy pre-flight training. Mack Smith was one of those, but I was not. The rest of us were divided into four groups, and sent on to V-12 college training.

Our group awoke one Sunday morning in March of 1944 in our Pullman car, which had been switched onto a siding of the Cotton Belt line in a remote part of southern Arkansas. In mid-morning, an old school bus pulled up on the dusty gravel road that adjoined the tracks. We piled our sea bags on top of it, and were hauled off to Arkansas A&M College near Monticello, where we would spend the next fourteen months. Two events, both athletic in nature, stand out. Once again I partici- pated in varsity basketball during an abbrevi- ated sea- son, and later that year I was matched up with B i l l Cromer in one of Lieutenant H o m e r Cole's Fri- day night boxing

Basketball remained a part of my life at Arkansas A & M College during my Navy V-12 schooling at that institution, now the University of Arkansas at Monticello. Members of that team, back row, left to right, Colbert, Vaughan, Gifford, and Fleck. Front row, Pabian, Lawson, Ray, and Thomas.

"smokers." Neither of us knew a thing about boxing, which my father had dubbed "a brute sport," and we flailed away at each other for the required seemingly endless three rounds.

The following year we were transferred to a Naval ROTC train- ing unit at the University of Oklahoma at Norman. Our Navy unit won the All-University Choral Singing Competition that year, and my basketball career ended with severe blisters on my feet. It was a sad day when I had to withdraw as a member of Bruce Drake's squad, especially since OU was scheduled to play both Long Island University and Adolph Rupp's UK later that year. They lost the Ken- tucky game, but defeated LIU. Coach Iba's A&M Cowboys repeated as NCAA champions, but the following year, Coach Drake's Sooners made it all the way to the finals, losing to Holy Cross, 58 - 47.

In due course, our group became the last wartime class to receive commissions as ensigns in the Naval Reserve. Rather than remain in the service, I chose a release to inactive duty, but remained active long enough to be promoted to lieutenant junior grade. When I returned to complete my B.A. at Norman that fall, I continued to wear my uniform on two occasions in order to qualify for a serviceman's half-fare on trips to and

A newly-commissioned ensign in the U. S. Naval Reserve.

from the university. It was on the first such trip that I met my future bride, Wanda Lee Rice, by far the best thing that ever happened to me.

Chapter Six
After the War

How do I love thee?
Let me count the ways…
                    —*Browning*

I had seen her pretty face in the window of a photography shop on Boyd Street, next to the house where I lived. On this particular occasion at the train terminal in Oklahoma City, I was serving as a sort of unofficial interpreter and guide for a group of five undergraduates from Baranquilla, Colombia, who were studying geology at OU. We lived in the same house, and since I now had a minor in Spanish, they had begun to rely on me to help them understand our difficult language. My Colombian friends were concerned about finding their

Wanda Lee Rice and I met at Oklahoma University in 1946 and were married three years later. This is the photo that caught my eye in the photographer's window at Norman before we had been introduced.

train when they transferred at the Saint Louis station, which at that time handled hundreds of passenger trains daily.

As luck would have it, Wanda Lee was also at the terminal on her way to her home in Arkansas, and she was traveling with her friend Gloria and Gloria's friend, George Souris, with whom I had worked on *The Sooner Hoist*, a navy publication. George introduced us, and we played bridge until we reached Springfield, where Wanda Lee changed trains. I helped her with her luggage, went on my way to St. Louis, guided my Colombian friends to their train, and then continued on to Cincinnati. On this particular trip my first stop would be in Dayton to visit my brother George, who, along with Warren Music, rented a room from our mutual friend from Van Lear, Harold Rucker and his wife Audria. That visit is marked in my memory by a single event. One morning, after George and Warren had departed for their factory jobs, Audria was stricken with labor pains, and Harold had to take her to the hospital where she would give birth to Mike, leaving me to finish bathing and diapering their

Richard Sparks astride his pony around 1934, several years prior to our visit with his brother, Doctor O. D. Sparks, at Leatherwood. At the left is their cousin Helen Harris (VLHS 1940), and at the right, their sister Darlene (VLHS 1947).

first-born, Sherrie, something I had never done before. After Mike arrived on the scene, I continued on to eastern Kentucky and visited my good friend Richard Sparks, who had also been released from active duty with the Navy.

When I arrived in Van Lear I could tell that things just weren't the same, neither the town nor the people. There were visible signs that the town's days as a productive coal mining center were numbered. We drove around town and I could see that the Company no longer kept the houses painted. Even the buildings and equipment at Number 5 mine seemed neglected. Richard told me that his brother, O.D., had been hired as the company physician by Blue Diamond Coal Company at Leatherwood, a brand new mining town near Hazard. We decided we would go visit Leatherwood's new doctor. Richard drove one of his dad's trucks and I rode shotgun.

During our visit, O.D. showed us around the new town, which was still in the building stage, with two camps planned, one in Perry County and another across the mountain near Cumberland in Harlan County. We could tell that O.D. was proud of the place. The following day, we drove over to another, older coal town, and our visit there convinced us that *our* town had been a much better place for two boys like us. There was trash everywhere, along the creek bank, up the hollows, and in and around every house. We stopped and talked with one little boy. He was dressed in ragged overalls, and he was barefoot. When we were that age, we dressed that way sometimes, but our moms always insisted that we wear clean clothes, and we could tell that this kid had been in the same clothes for weeks, if not all summer long, and he looked like he may not have had much to eat lately, so we shared a candy bar with him, and then went on back to O.D.'s house, one of the newer company houses, perched high atop a hill. When we told him about the boy and his town, O.D. said that there were several such towns nearby, and it was his hope that he could help make Leatherwood, especially the main camp, into a better place than any of those, or, as he put it, "more like Van Lear used to be."

After we ate supper that last night, O.D. seemed to sense that Richard and I were both very much interested in the history of our town, and he began to dredge up things from his memory, things he thought would be of interest to us. He told us about old Van Lear. He said that Jack Price came to Consol's Miller's Creek town from Somerset, Pennsylvania, in 1917 as an assistant to the mine manager, Garner Fletcher. Later, when Mister Price assumed the manager's job, Van Lear became widely known as a wonderful place to live and work. As O.D. told it, Price was the man who set the standards for others to follow. He carefully screened the men and families who were employed in the town. He brought in good teachers from back East and demanded high standards from them and the Van Lear schools, which were attended by his own nieces and

Members of this award-winning Safety Team are, left to right, Tobe Fairchild, Dewey May, Gene Auxier (VLHS 1928), Bernard Greer, and Howard Painter. Kneeling at the front is Joe Sarsfield, team captain. Despite rigorous training in safety procedures, and regular inspection of the mines, methane gas sometimes collected in pockets and went undetected until an explosion like that of July 17, 1935, occurred, instantly killing nine Van Lear miners. On another July day, sixty-seven years later, nine miners entrapped in a mine near Somerset, Pennsylvania, were rescued unharmed, thanks, in part at least, to more efficient recovery equipment and methods. Despite these advances, it is doubtful that Van Lear's nine miners could have been saved.

nephews and the children of all the management people. Miners were expected to send their children to school, and those who didn't were soon dismissed from their jobs.

"Safety first" became more than a buzzword or slogan, O.D. told us. Those words were found on printed signs that were hung everywhere, both in and outside the mines, he said. All of the men who worked in and around the mines were taught how to practice safety, first and foremost, before attempting even the simplest operations. In routinely scheduled safety meetings, workers were taught the proper way to lift heavy objects, how to maneuver around potentially lethal high-voltage electric lines, and how to handle explosives and dangerous machinery safely. Disaster procedures were worked out and ingrained in the minds and habits of each worker. Periodic safety meets were held in which teams from neighboring mining towns competed with local teams for speed and expertness in dealing with simulated mining accidents.

When O.D. told us this, I recalled George getting all decked out

Superintendent C.V. Snapp and faculty, c. 1926. Bess Bradley stands next to Mister Snapp. My first-grade teacher, Susie Risner, is second from the right in the second row.

in white pants, white shirt, and tie, and taking part in those safety meets and, after winning a local meet, going with his team to compete at Fairmont, West Virginia. As a result of this attention to proper mining techniques, the Van Lear mines under Jack Price had a safety record unequaled anywhere. The mine accident that took my father's life and the lives of the eight others had occurred well after Price's departure. Despite this one dark blemish, Richard and I were proud that we had been privileged to live in Van Lear.

"There were men's choirs under School Superintendent C.V. Snapp," O.D. told us, "and a town orchestra, and visits by Lyceum groups." As for athletic teams, O.D. said the Van Lear town baseball team was usually one of the best on Big Sandy.

"When Jack Price moved on to better himself in 1928, a gala celebration was held with dignitaries from Fairmont, Pittsburgh, and Baltimore," he said. "There was dancing and fireworks that lasted far into the night."

I didn't remember anything about that big event, but I did recall seeing a special train that backed into town with a half-dozen flatcars, each draped with white bunting, and men in dress suits, seated on chairs, gazing out at our town as though they were visiting a zoo and we were the monkeys. When Richard's brother told us about the celebration, I remembered the train, but nothing else about that event. O.D. told us that there had been a huge banquet in the Club House, with champagne and oysters, iced down in barrels in special box cars, and strange and exotic kinds of food that was hardly ever seen in our part of the world. The celebration was capped off the following day with a Sunday double header baseball game which, I'm sure, Van Lear must have won.

O.D. said that the stories about these things had left a lasting impression on him. As a result of seeing and hearing the town orchestra during his boyhood, he took up the cornet and became a member of a town band. Because of the good medical doctors in our town, O.D. decided to go to medical school and become a doctor. After a brief tour of duty at Leatherwood, he moved on into a private practice in nearby London, Kentucky. Doctor Lay took his place at Leatherwood.

When Richard and I began our return journey the next morning, we talked about the things his brother had told us. We marveled over "the Van Lear that used to be" and wondered if those "good old days" would ever return.

Upon my return to the OU campus, Wanda Lee and I had several dates, but money was short. Although our paths did cross on other occasions, I carefully hoarded my slim finances, got by mostly on the GI bill and a couple of small loans from George, and supplemented this with kitchen work for my landlady, Mrs. Smith. Just prior to my graduation, I began to scan the bulletin boards for notices advertising employment opportunities. I chose two interviews, the first with a representative from Kobe Incorporated, an oil-drilling equipment and engineering company, and the second with Armstrong Cork Company, the linoleum people from Lancaster, Pennsylvania.

I interviewed with Armstrong, fancying myself as a potential cork buyer for that firm in Spain, since I had some facility with the language, but J. Ed. Smith, their personnel manager, told me that the advertised job openings had been closed since Generalisimo Franco faced another possible revolution in that country. He sent me instead to an interview with George Kittridge, who was seeking factory reps for the company's floor division. Both Kobe and Armstrong offered me jobs, and I consulted Cousin Harry Howell, who had accepted a position as vice-president in charge of Ford Motor Company's forging operations in Canton, Ohio. He favored Kobe, and with my B.A. in math and physics I did seem better suited to this sort of industry, but I opted for Armstrong, feeling this kind of employer would be most likely to help me meet a personal need for skill and poise in social situations. Besides, the eastern states had always been more appealing to me than the West or Midwest. There was another factor at play, one that I had never acknowledged, even to myself. During my senior year I had enrolled in a course in creative writing, which was taught by Elizabeth Holman, and it was in that class that I realized my real interest and aptitude lay in language arts, not math and science. At that time, Armstrong Cork Company had a multi-talented man named Cameron Hawley at the head of its advertising department. There were no immediate openings in his department, but I somehow felt that I could advance my interest in writing and advertising by affiliating with such a company.

Following four months' training in Lancaster, I was sent down to Atlanta, and assigned the Tennessee-North Georgia-Alabama territory under the supervision of Bob Gardner. Wanda Lee and I had kept up an on-again, off-again correspondence. On one of my visits to Nashville I happened to pick up the *Nashville Banner*, and there was her photograph, with an accompanying article concerning her appearance in a play at Nashville's Community Playhouse. I surprised her by showing up that evening, and we went out to dinner the next two days, and agreed to become "engaged." Three months later, on the fourteenth of February in 1949, we were married at First Baptist Church in Paragould, Arkansas, with the reverend D.C. Applegate officiating. We then moved into a small apartment on Compton Street, just down the hill from the WSM tower and transmitter in Nashville.

Now I would be remiss if I failed to tell you that I left the directors at the Community Playhouse sorely disappointed when I spirited off their protégé. One of the directors, Raymond Johnson, was a friend of Helen Hayes, and he had all but finalized plans for my bride to join the First Lady of the American Theatre as her roommate and understudy at the Old Vic in London. Wanda Lee's last roommate in Nashville was Jean Spiegel, who would soon become the bride of Harold Beckholdt. They would go on to New York, and then to Hollywood, where Harold would change his name to Rance Howard in hopes that this would better his chances of getting roles in cowboy movies. It seemed to work. Not only did Harold and Jean find work, they produced two sons who also excelled in films.

Their eldest son Ron Howard went on to become Opie on "The Andy Griffith Show," and later a well-respected Oscar-winning director, and his brother Clint also did some outstanding film and TV work. William Dennis Weaver, with whom Wanda Lee had worked at OU, became Chester on "Gunsmoke," and other members of the OU School of Drama also had success in the theatre.

My own personal interests lay more in the direction of broadcasting and writing. One day Art Smith, the son of one of my flooring clients in Chattanooga, suggested that his friend Bob Rounsaville could use our services at a radio station in Louisville, Kentucky. Wanda Lee became a bookkeeper, and I an account executive at WLOU, the first racially integrated radio station in Kentucky. A year later, Bob asked me to be the manager of his newly acquired station in Miami, and we spent the next two years there with WMBM, which was that state's second racially mixed broadcast facility. Our broadcasting format soon took on cosmopolitan tones as we had programs devoted to Jewish, Chinese, Hungarian, and Polish ethnic and cultural groups, in addition to black and white sports and general information programming. We carried horse racing from all three South Florida tracks and featured numerous "celebrity" type shows, but found it difficult to build an audience. I was re-introduced to racial intolerance when one of our disk jockeys, Clarence McDaniels, known as "The Bronze Voice," was chased out of state by the South Miami police, who accused him of "stealing sod." My news director, Ed Cook, called me early that morning to tell me what had happened. When we visited the "scene of the crime" we found our man's auto with a bullet hole in the windshield and sod piled in the back, but Ed told me that he had been there earlier in the morning, and there was no sod anywhere in or around the car. McDaniels later turned up in New York, unharmed, but this news reached us only after local entertainers, including Martha Raye, held a benefit for our man's "widow." Clarence remained in New York under the protective cover of Walter White and the NAACP. In the competitive world of South Florida, we soon realized that we neither liked the prospect of my dying from a stress-induced heart attack at a young age, nor did we particularly care for the year-long tropical season.

Our lives were shaken in December of 1954 when word reached us that my boyhood friend Richard Sparks had died, shortly after his marriage to a young lady from Nicholasville, Kentucky. Word reached us after the funeral during my final year in Florida.

When Wanda Lee's father became ill, we decided to go to Arkansas and try our hands at farming. Of the four years that I farmed in partnership with my father-in-law—1955, 1956, 1957, and 1958—only one was free of drought, and even that one year

Richard Sparks, shortly before his untimely death in 1951.

was marred with low commodity prices. In 1957, Wanda Lee started teaching in the local school, I began teaching at Hoxie the following year, and she joined me there a year later. The Hoxie school system was the second public system to end racial segregation in the state of Arkansas. With our prior service in racially mixed radio, it now seemed that we had somehow been destined to play a role in breaking down racial barriers, although, quite frankly, neither of us ever gave this much thought, one way or the other. To us it was "the thing to do."

The next ten years were among our happiest, as we continued to work for the Hoxie school district, Wanda Lee as a speech and drama teacher, and I as teacher, and later as principal of the high school. Although I enjoyed the principal's work, it was as a teacher that I found more satisfaction. Early in my teaching career another series of events occurred, leading to yet another change. I had been asked by the state supervisor of math instruction to evaluate a math workshop at Jonesboro. Shortly afterwards I began to investigate the linear programming techniques taught by B.F. Skinner of Harvard, and I soon learned that his methods were very effective in the classroom, particularly when I used a roll of acetate and an over-head projector. In this manner I could stand at the front of the room, facing my students, and observe their reactions as they stumbled and then recovered as a result of something that I would "program" into a particular algebraic sequence or procedure. These "lapses," I learned, occurred quite frequently on a single page, since interim steps were often omitted by the textbook writer, usually because of limitations on the number of pages the publisher could devote to the book. It was all of these missing parts that I began to provide on my acetate screen.

Eventually, I learned that my classroom methods were a marketable commodity, and I began to have success writing programmed instructional materials, both in mathematics, and later, when I acquired sufficient skill, in language arts and vocational trades. Among some of the more successful materials were such things as "Mr. Phun Phonics" and "Ceres: A Space Odyssey," the latter recommended in one of NASA's early catalogs as a useful disk for early Apple computers.

Although I enjoyed teaching as much or more than anything I had ever done, writing and publishing instructional materials held out the opportunity to continue teaching while earning more money, an all too frequent occurrence in the lives of good public school teachers. I regretted leaving the Hoxie school, but took some satisfaction in the knowledge that we had improved the learning atmosphere in the high school, where we had four National Merit semi-finalists and winners of three National Merit Scholarships and state speech and journalism award winners as well.

Throughout our married lives, Wanda Lee and I always made it a point to return to Van Lear at least once each year. On our first visit from our home in Nashville in 1949, my longtime friend Richard Sparks took us over to John's Creek, where the Corps of Engineers had started constructing an earthen dam three years earlier and had recently begun impounding Dewey Lake. Richard told us that the lake would revitalize the area's now-flagging economy, and some had hopes that the mines might reopen. The former proved correct, but the mines had no rebirth. As we continued to make these visits, Wanda Lee learned to love the town and its people every bit as much as I. Together, we made a sort of unspoken commitment to do what we could for the town, both in honor of souls who once lived there, and for ourselves and those who would follow. And so I began my research into what had transpired after I departed.

Consolidation Coal Company had announced as early as April 2, 1946, that it would sell all of its real estate in Van Lear. In retrospect, a life of thirty-six years seemed woefully short, particularly for the town I had known as a young boy, but as I was to learn later, this same fate awaited many such company-built towns in America. By 1951, virtually all of the company-owned town where I had spent most of my youth, was sold off and abandoned, with current renters getting first-refusal rights to purchase their homes. Many of them did just that, while some opted not to buy property, thus opening up the opportunity for others to acquire additional houses, company buildings, and pieces of land. Many improved their property, and the town seemed to flourish for a time, even winning an award in the mid-1960s, but the place soon became a mixed bag, with some owners taking great pride in the appearances of their property, and others allowing theirs to fall into disrepair. During the thirty-year period from 1951 to 1981, most of the major structures, including all five coal tipples and shop buildings, the hotel, and school houses, were torn down, the recreation building and clubhouse burned; and Van Lear was in danger of losing its reputation as having once been one of Kentucky's premier coal towns. The leadership void left by the departure of Company management personnel was being felt in ways that were not always obvious to residents. A regressive property tax also contributed to the malaise, encouraging not only negative growth, but abandonment of property as well. When the people voted out incorporation the decline continued.

In 1980, my friend John Allen suggested that, with my background in both broadcasting and education, I might be a likely candidate for an appointment to the Arkansas Educational Television Commission. Frank White, a Republican, had been elected governor, unseating Bill Clinton, and John had long been a tireless worker in Republican Party politics. Although I had always been apolitical, I agreed that this was probably the only kind of government appointment that would be of interest to me. Subsequently, I served a full eight-year term. Two years after my initial appointment, Bill Clinton regained his gubernatorial position, and although I had been appointed by his opponent, I was retained on the commission, and invited to join his task force on satellite education, chaired by his good friend, Diane Blair. I like to think that we "did some good" in our appointive capacities, and indeed satellite downlinks were soon made available to a number of public schools, thanks to our groundwork and funding from the state's Rural Electric Administration.

During my high school career, we had appropriated the format of the old "GE College Bowl" and modified it into what we called "The Beta Bowl," an academic competition between opposing teams, which we staged as an assembly program in the Hoxie gymnasium. It had proved to be highly popular, and I saw no good reason why we shouldn't use our statewide ETV network to do something similar. Kentucky and a few other states were already doing it. My suggestion at first met with a stony reception from my fellow commissioners, and from our new ETV director Raymond Ho as well. In fairness, I must report that the only individual who endorsed it was

Hillary Clinton, and it was at her urging that AETN commenced an annual scholastic competition known as "The Governor's Quiz Bowl," which continues to this day, preceded by spirited competition in statewide regional playoffs.

Meanwhile, the minority shareholder in my instructional materials company, who had seen to the printing and marketing of our material, had begun to devote more and more time to his tennis-playing sons. At the same time, I began to pay more attention to Van Lear, and we soon ended our business relationship. I sold off the assets, and formed a new, less formal company, whose needs would allow me more time to spend on things of a less demanding and more interesting, if less remunerative, nature. After twenty years as a writer of instructional materials, I was "burned out," a phenomenon shared by many who devote themselves to a single task without sufficient diversity, and I felt the need to do something else. During that 1964 - 1984 period, however, I had diverted myself from the sometimes stressful demands of constantly writing under deadlines by constructing a scale model of my old hometown, and I had begun to spend a great deal of my time on that and other such activities, particularly a writing project on company-owned towns and their ultimate fate. Of course, Van Lear was uppermost among them in my mind.

Chapter Seven

A Town Remembered

I have eaten your bread and salt,
I have drunk your water and wine;
the deaths ye died I have watched beside,
and the lives that ye led were mine.
—*Rudyard Kipling*

Before I knew it, thirty years had passed since I brought Wanda Lee on her first visit to Van Lear. During that time, we rarely missed making annual trips to attend family reunions, initially at Ashland's Central Park and, after 1976, at Jenny Wiley State Resort Park near Prestonsburg, just over a few ridges from Van Lear. My later years had shown me worlds previously unknown to me, an erstwhile lad from the eastern Kentucky coalfields, yet I found it hard to resist going back to the town that seemed to hold an almost magnetic attraction for me and my wife, who had also bonded with the town and many of its good people. In 1980 I returned from a business trip to learn that Doris Harris Smith had called to tell us that she and Iris Ward Blair wanted to have a school reunion. When I telephoned Christina Wetzel Stapleton I learned that she knew nothing about a reunion, but on the appointed day she, her husband Edgar, and her brother-in-law Odell, joined us at the Highland Restaurant, where we met with Doris, Iris, Jim Preston, Jim Ward, and Betty Brickley Ward, most of us somewhat confused as to what we were about, but glad to see each other again. After that informal gathering, Christina decided we should have a "real" school reunion. Long active with Eastern Star, Chris knew how to get things done. She recruited her daughter Kaye, her husband Ed, her sister-in-law Mary Rucker Stapleton, and her niece Nicky Pelphrey, to help her get things organized. In August of 1981, about 250 former students and graduates of Van Lear High School attended Van Lear's first-ever school reunion at Johnson Central High School in Paintsville.

At this time my small educational media firm had added video to its audio and print activities. Encouraged by the turnout of people, I thought that there was enough interest in the "Van Lear that used to be" to warrant the production of a video documentary, providing I could find enough old photographs to copy, and old-timers to interview. Christina Stapleton put me in touch with Jeanette Knowles, a Van Learite of recent vintage, in-

This three-part composite photo shows some of the early powers behind the Van Lear reunion movement. At the top are Doris Harris Smith (VLHS 1944), Jim Preston (VLHS 1946), and Naomi Rucker Williams (VLHS 1942). At the far right in the middle photo is Christina Wetzel Stapleton (VLHS 1932). Pictured below is Jeanette Knowles.

terested in the town's history. Upon learning about Silva Lyon and his cache of old photos, Wanda Lee and I returned to Van Lear in 1982, where we assembled a group of people who were willing to be interviewed about the town and their experiences there. Silva and his wife Fannie came from Frankfort, Cousin Beulah Hammond Williamson from Ashland, Virgil Porter from Lexington, C.V. Snapp from Jenkins, and Verne Horne, Dr. Paul B. Hall, and others from Paintsville and environs. In addition to Silva, a number of other people also brought old photographs, which we copied for later use in the video.

For the video, I licensed generic background music, and attempted to obtain permission to use Loretta Lynn's recording of "Blue Kentucky Girl" in her part of the story. In pursuing this goal I first called her (then) manager, David Skepner. At his behest, I wrote a rather long and detailed letter on August 6, 1981 in which I described our plans and those of the soon-to-be organized Van Lear Historical Society. Time passed with no response. Then, just as I was in the process of making the final edit and adding a sound track prior to our showing of the video at the second school reunion, a representative of Loretta's music-licensing agency called from California to tell me that Skepner would grant permission to the historical society, but not to an individual. Unfortunately, I had to tell them that the society was still in the process of being formed. As a result we had to go ahead without Loretta's music. Instead, I hired local musicians, including Grand Ole Opry banjoist-fidler Tim Crouch, to record background instrumental music for the soundtrack. Others on that track were Tim Arnold, percussion; McKinley Burge, dobro; Max Burge, bass; Donnie Murphy, harmonica; and Leon Tidwell, guitar, all excellent Arkansas musicians, and the equal of many professionals in Nashville.

We returned to eastern Kentucky a second time in 1982 to show our initial video footage, and it was at this meeting that the non-profit Van Lear Historical Society was organized. At that gathering, former Van Lear School Superintendent Verne P. Horne nominated

Jim Preston as the society's first president, and a separate school reunion committee headed by Nicky Pelphrey made plans for an even bigger reunion. The next year (1983) seven to eight hundred former townspeople filled one side of the Johnson Central gymnasium. There, amidst much happy noise and confusion, we showed our video, *Van Lear: A Town Remembered*, and the Bankmule spirit was revived. It was obvious that I was not the only one who had

Verne P. Horne, our former school superintendent, who helped organize the Van Lear Historical Society and who remembered the organization in his will.

Jim Preston (VLHS 1946), who was nominated by Verne Horne as the first president of the Van Lear Historical Society.

good feelings about the old hometown. In the years that followed, well-attended town reunions would be held annually, with school reunions on alternate years.

The year of the "big" reunion, Charles Spears, former Chessie System Yardmaster at Paintsville and a Van Learite, prevailed on his bosses to donate an old C&O caboose to the VLHS. Jim Bowling, Jim DeLong, Gary Trimble, and Danny Blair laid ties and lengths of track in the old railbed across from the site of the high school and, on October 15, 1983, volunteers Ray Pennington, Bruce

Charles Spears (VLHS 1945), at the right, was largely responsible for obtaining the C&O caboose for the new Van Lear minipark.

A crowd gathers at the caboose in 1985 to hear Dr. Paul B. Hall tell about his Van Lear experiences.

Teamus Bowling (VLHS 1942) descends the steps at the caboose as his wife Pauline and I look on.

Castle, Billy Ward, Bob Justice, Ova Salyer, and William Hannah borrowed a low-boy, a truck, and two end-loaders, and placed the caboose onto its final resting place. Volunteer work by Bill Rucker and other VLHS members refurbished the caboose to house the video and other memorabilia, and to serve as a centerpiece for a recreational mini-park. The Bankmule spirit had not only been re-discovered, but was now showing signs of being renewed.

In January of 1984, the first issue of *The Bankmule*, official news-letter of the society, was put together by Jeanette Knowles, Danny Blevins, and other talented residents. It continues to this day as a quarterly sent out to more than 600 members who make a modest $10 annual donation to VLHS. Those early issues began to tell the story of Van Lear's past, provided a means for former residents to recall and celebrate the part that they and their families had played in the town's life and development, and served as a link to its present and future citizens.

Citizens National Bank President O.T. Dorton presents the deed to the old Consol office building to the Van Lear Historical Society. Left to right, Phyllis Blevins, President Dorton, O.W. Harris (VLHS 1935), then-VLHS-president Bill Rucker, Danny Blevins (VLHS 1958), Dennis Dorton, Joyce McCallister Meade (VLHS 1954), and Jessica Blevins.

Teamus Bowling and I in front of the old office building shortly after it was acquired by the historical society. Numerous alterations to the original structure had been made by its prior owner, and the building was in obvious need of restorative work.

On April 23, 1984, Citizens National Bank of Paintsville gave the old Consolidation Coal Company office building to the society. President O.T. Dorton made the title transfer, stating, "We are committed to preserving the history of our area, and this building is important in the history of Van Lear." Plans went forward for the restoration of the old building as the society's headquarters and as a center for other community activities. Later issues of *The Bankmule* featured news of this and other advances made by the historical society.

The office building at Van Lear, c. 1920, when it was owned and maintained by the Consolidation Coal Company. After the Citizens National Bank gave the building to the Van Lear Historical Society in the mid 1980s, that non-profit group began to attempt to restore it to its original condition. A miners' museum now occupies the second floor, and the model of the town is on the third floor.

During my twenty-year career as a writer of educational materials, I worked mostly in my major field of mathematics. Toward the close of that period, I wrote several things in the social studies field, one of which centered around an investigation of small company-built towns in America. As I became more and more interested in the activities of the fledgling Van Lear Historical Society, this work evolved into a little book that I would eventually title *Blue Moon Over Kentucky: A Biography of Kentucky's Troubled High-*

lands. The choice of that title was not made without some thought given to it. To me, Van Lear was a "once in a great while" kind of place, not unlike a "blue moon," the term used to describe a second full moon within a single month, a rare event. Then, too, I felt that the title accurately represented my feelings of both happiness and sadness about my old hometown, reflecting its once joyful past, and its decline and uncertain future. As I researched and wrote, Wanda Lee painted a picture of the old Number 5 mine tipple for the book's cover. When I completed the little book in 1985, I donated a substantial number of copies to the Van Lear Historical Society as a fund-raiser.

Governor Martha Layne Collins accepts a copy of Blue Moon *from Silva Lyon, 1985.*

Before I began building a scale model of my hometown in 1958, I wrote to Consolidation Coal Company offices about my project, and I soon received a lengthy and cordial reply from J. B. Feather, sales promotion manager for Consol. "Your letter," he said, "brings back fond memories of our Van Lear Division which, in 40 years with the Company, I have visited several times." He enclosed some excellent photographs for use in designing my model, and a month later he wrote again, commenting, "It would be a great day for Van Lear if a firm or firms should ever decide to bring their industries to that area. We are sorry we cannot share with you the hope that Van Lear will rise again, in our time anyway. There are a great number of incentives for industry to locate there, and someday this could very well come to pass."

Eleven years passed, and my work on my model of the town continued as a part-time diversion. Roger M. Haynes, manager of personnel for Consol, wrote to me in January of 1969, and put me in touch with David Zegeer, then division superintendent of Bethlehem Mines Corporation at Jenkins, Kentucky, and with Sam Cassidy, who had been responsible for Consol's Millers Creek Division. In a letter to Mr. Haynes, Mr. Cassidy remarked, "Van Lear was one of the better mining towns, well laid-out, not crowded, a broad enough valley, and there was an excellent community spirit. This resulted in well-kept, clean houses and towns.... I am amazed and delighted that Mr. Vaughan is interested in constructing a three-dimensional model of the town. I was through Van Lear last summer, and it still looks good."

A follow-up to Mr. Haynes' letter brought a friendly response from David A. Zegeer in which he told me that one of his men re-called taking a carload of photographs and records to Consol's Pocahontas, Virginia, office in 1956 or 1957, but nothing further came from my efforts to locate any of the Company's photos or records. By 1981, most of the old middle-management personnel with Consol had retired, and my later inquiries brought forth nothing that would be of help in completing the model. It was then that Chris Stapleton told me about Jeanette Knowles and her interest in Van Lear history. It was Jeanette who put me in touch with Silva Lyon who, along with Peggy Beers, Peggy's Aunt Bertha McKay and a few others, loaned some excellent photographs, which aided me in com-

Peggy Beers and Jon Kelly visit during a school reunion. Peggy helped round up photos for use in the Van Lear video documentary.

pleting the model and, later, the book and video. By the early 1980s, not only had many of the old Consol people departed, but Consol itself had been absorbed by the energy-conglomerate CONOCO— Continental Oil Company—which, in turn, would be absorbed into the duPont organization, whereupon it seemed to me that all traces of the friendliness and helpfulness that had once characterized Consol vanished almost completely.

Shortly after completing the model, Wanda Lee and I visited Garnetta and Russell (Bill) Rucker, who was then serving as president of the Van Lear Historical Society. I casually remarked that, if they ever decided to create a miners' museum in the old office building, I would donate my model of Van Lear. In May of 1984 I sent Bill and Elmo Burke detailed drawings of the model and a letter detailing its design. In March of 1989, Bill called me. "Buddy," he said, "we're ready for your model." Wanda Lee and I had retired, and in early May we were planning a trip to the British Isles with our dear friend and former student, Mary Poe, and her husband, Bobby. Then in our sixties, we decided that it was now or never, and so I dismantled the thirty-foot-long model, sawed the base into eight huge pieces, rented a U-Haul, and carefully packed the delicate scale-model structures. We then set out for Kentucky.

Elmo Burke, an excellent draftsman, had built a foundation and backdrop for the scale model. Unfortunately, Elmo died while working on it. Upon our arrival, we learned that B.B. Kretzer would supervise a group of young men who were serving time with the Johnson County Detention Center for minor infractions of law, and they would assist us in rebuilding our model. Also on hand to lend their valuable assistance were Warren Harris, Charles and Billie Spears, Bill and Garnetta Rucker, Betty Brickley

The late Elmo Burke (VLHS 1941) who suffered a fatal heart attack while constructing the base and backdrop for the Van Lear model.

Ward and her daughter, and several other local people. During the next ten days, we were able to put the model together on the third floor of the old office building, where it has become one of the museum's main attractions. Wanda Lee's painting, which we used for the cover of the *Blue Moon* book, now hangs in the museum, across from the town model.

Since the Van Lear Historical Society was first organized in 1982,

A section of the town model, showing a portion of the midtown area in Van Lear as it appeared in the 1930s.

In this view of the town model, the Sparks' home is at the upper left and Cassels' to the right. Our house was the first one-story cottage below and to the right. A horse-drawn coal wagon may be visible in the foreground.

its own history has been marked with some success and more than a few setbacks, despite the best efforts of a small cadre of volunteer workers. The society succeeded in preserving the old office building and in gathering a growing collection of family and personal artifacts. At the same time, hundreds of former residents have contributed to the lore and history of the community with their own personal memories of the town.

Throughout its early history as the owner-operator of the town and mines at Van Lear, Consolidation Coal Company brought in people of quality to live and work there. This emphasis on quality began with management, and extended to labor and ancillary service personnel, including members of the medical profession

When Silva Lyon's family came to Van Lear, they were greeted by these Millers Creek Railroad personnel. At the top, Bill Bradley, Tan Whitaker, Bill Condon, Estill Daniel, John Carroll, and Emmit Poole stand on the cowcatcher of the locomotive; in the middle is the 2-car passenger train that brought the Lyons to Van Lear; and, the third scene is that of a group gathered around a much larger coal train locomotive.

and those who taught in the town's schools. All of these things were affirmed by the people we interviewed for our video documentary.

Silva Lyon told us that his father Doctor John Lyon brought his family to Van Lear shortly after the town was built. He remained

Photos of the 1918 era comprise this three-part composite. At the top is a group of miners at Mine No. 155; in the center is a parade in front of the home occupied by the family of Doctor John Lyon; and the lower scene shows a large crowd at a Fourth of July celebration at the playground near Bradley Crossing.

there as one of two company doctors, attending to the medical needs of Van Lear people from 1916 until 1928. In his interview Silva, like many who spent their formative years in Van Lear, spoke of the many fond memories that he had of those early days. His comments also revealed something about the dedication of the medical personnel and the quality of life there.

"Father came there in the spring of 1916," he recalled. "He returned to Ashland in June to get the family. We traveled by passenger train from Ashland, changing to the Millers Creek Railroad at West Van Lear Junction. There were two coaches on that line. I remember that they stopped to let us off right in front of our house, the only one at the time that had been built next to the Baptist Church and the lot where they were planning to build a high school. That particular house had just been vacated by Herb Queen, Consol's construction superintendent, who had moved to Louisa.

"Doctor James C. Sparks was the first physician hired by the company, and father was the second. They actually worked for the miners in that the medical fees were withheld from the payroll—a reasonable amount, as I recall—and most of this was turned over to the doctors and the dentist, who then provided and paid for their own medicine and equipment. Even so, I'm sorry to say, the doctor sometimes got the short end of the stick.

"At first, father rode a horse to make his rounds. This was back when doctors made house calls. The railroad stretched the length of the town, and father later bought and used a railroad-cycle which he pedaled up and down the five-mile length of Millers Creek. When he reached a patient's house, he lifted the machine off the track, took his black bag, and spent whatever time was necessary to minister to the needs of the sick. Later, in 1921, he bought one of the first automobiles in Van Lear, a wire-wheeled baby Overland, and this made travel somewhat easier, although there were places he couldn't drive."

Silva told us how his father and family returned to Ashland in 1928 when Doctor Lyon joined the Stevenson Hospital. He died there of a cerebral hemorrhage on the 29th day of December in 1929, a month short of his forty-sixth birthday.

"It isn't just because he was my father," Silva told us, "but if there ever was a man that lived a clean life, that was him. He had no bad habits that I knew of other than working too hard. He would go sometimes for several days at a time and never go to bed. He would sit in a chair and nod off for a while. Many a person has told me about his coming and staying all night with their sick loved ones."

John Lewis and his Ashland band on the lawn of the Van Lear Rec building, around 1924.

Silva spoke of the quality of life in Van Lear when he was a young man growing up there. "My introduction to light opera was at Van Lear," he recalled. "The United Lyceum Bureau brought us several light operatic programs. Cleveland Chambers was manager of the new recreation building. He and other managers who followed him were encouraged to book higher type programs. I recall we had musical programs that featured both local and outside talent. John Lewis taught instrumental music at Van Lear. After he moved to Ashland, he returned often with his bands for holiday concerts. I remember Bill Hess and Bob Jasper played instruments in a local orchestral group."

Silva Lyon told us about his brother, Ernest, who got his start in music at Van Lear and Jenkins. "He later completed a doctorate and taught music at the University of Louisville," Silva said. "There may have been some things that we could have found in the larger cities, but the community offered us just about everything."

Christina Wetzel Stapleton echoed those remarks when asked about her impressions of life at Van Lear during the 1930s. Chris and her husband, Edgar Stapleton, remained in Van Lear after their marriage. "I don't think I missed a thing," she said. "We had everything then. The school offered a wide variety of activities. I don't think there was a week that someone wasn't presenting a

Christina Wetzel Stapleton (VLHS 1932), her daughter Kaye (VLHS 1961), and niece Nickey Wetzel Pelphrey (VLHS 1954) are largely responsible for commencing and continuing the biannual Van Lear School reunions. Pictured at the top are Chris and her husband Edgar (VLHS 1931), both of whom have actively supported the town and its activities. In the middle photo, Jim Kelly (VLHS 1954), then-president of the historical society, interviews Marie Tuzy McCallister, recipient of the 1992 award for oldest widow of a Van Lear miner (Herschel McCallister). At left below, Manfred Pickrell (VLHS 1924) receives the award as the oldest graduate present in 1984. At the right, Tom Wills (VLHS 1953) presents the 1985 award to the oldest graduate to Silva Lyon (VLHS 1925), son of Doctor John Lyon, and the donor of many of the photos for the video, Van Lear: A Town Remembered.

play or musical program at the theatre in the recreation building. When the school wasn't having something, the churches organized an event. And we had chaperones, two or more couples. We young people didn't resent this. To us, this wasn't an intrusion. We were glad to have our parents along, for this meant that they were interested in us and our welfare. They accompanied us on wiener roasts or hay-rides, or swimming or camping trips, or perhaps to one of the out of town athletic events."

"We had lots of parties in private homes," Chris continued. "We celebrated birthdays, Halloween, many things. And there were always parents to chaperone us."

When Loretta Lynn's story, *Coal Miner's Daughter*, was mentioned, Chris was quick to remind us that it wasn't like that for those who lived in town. No one ever went hungry. "If times were hard and you had a crust of bread," she said, "others shared part of it. We didn't have a lot of money, but no one ever starved. I don't think I missed a thing. I've been here most of my life and I intend to stay here. When I leave Van Lear it will be under someone else's steam, and not my own."

Following this affirmation of her love for the town that had nurtured her and so many others, Chris made her most memorable commentary on the human condition, then and now. "I just wish the young people of today had the love and closeness we had back then," she said, with great feeling. "If they did, perhaps they wouldn't be using drugs and dope in this world in which they seem to be so unhappy." Christina passed away in September of 2001, a deeply felt loss to Kaye and Ed, and to countless others as well.

When I recalled the remarks of Silva Lyon concerning his love of the town, and the good works performed there by his father, Doctor Paul B. Hall eagerly acknowledged Doctor Lyon's dedication to his medical profession. "I never knew a finer man than Doctor John Lyon," Doctor Hall told me during our interview in 1982. "I got to know him during the terrible flu epidemic of 1918. At that time, I was a medical student at the University of Louisville. One

Beulah Hammond Williamson (VLHS 1926), her cousin George Vaughan (VLHS 1932), and Doctor Paul B. Hall visit during one of the Van Lear school reunions.

day I was called into the dean's office where I was told that I was being sent to Van Lear for a one-week seminar to learn how to treat the flu. That one week stretched into four. I never saw anything like it before or since. I would start at the power station at the river. Any house you would go into would have four or five people laid out like cordwood. Doctor Lyon was tireless. He seldom slept. I did the best I could. Some got well in spite of me."

Frank Harris, who had received two years' medical schooling, was hired that year to help care for those stricken with influenza. At that time, the eastern-most double house on Slate Row was outfitted and used as a hospital under the supervision of a visiting order of Catholic nuns.

Doctors Munn, Spencer, Shepherd, Wolfe, and Turner, and nurses Florence Beane and Virginia Beavers followed Doctors Sparks and Lyon in that same selfless tradition. Among the services offered were free medical and dental check-ups for the children and adults, a practice rarely found anywhere in the United States today.

Mrs. Jake Wills, Virginia Beavers, and Mrs. William Harrison serve as garden judges in the summer of 1927.

"I almost came to Van Lear after I graduated from medical school," Doctor Hall continued, recalling more of his past. "In fact, I was on my way there from Louisville when Doctor Holbrook met me on the train at Torchlight. He offered me more money and the chance to work in Tobe Rule's hospital, and so I went to Paintsville."

During his video interview, Doctor Hall was overly modest in his self-assessment of his medical prowess, both during his student-intern days when he ministered to flu-stricken Van Lear residents, and after receiving his medical degree. He became a leading figure in the region, and the Paul B. Hall Medical Center at Paintsville is named for him.

After he recounted his experience as a young medical student tending the victims of the 1918 flu epidemic, he turned his attention to baseball. "I almost became a professional baseball player," he said. "Pittsburgh offered me a contract." He said this with great pride, almost as though he would have preferred a career as a professional athlete, despite the fact that he acquired an enviable reputation in medicine. He played baseball for the University of Louisville and the University of Kentucky, earning a place in both schools' halls of fame, but it was his Van Lear experience that he recalled most vividly.

"When I played second base for Van Lear," he told us, "they gave me a job in the mines. They put a fellow who was baseball crazy in charge of me—Lawrence Meddings, a wonderful man— and he would take me to a place where the coal was high, and he would leave me there, safely out of the way until it was time to go outside for baseball practice."

When asked to comment once more about memories that he might have of Doctor John Lyon and Fred Vinson, Doctor Hall replied, "I never had better friends in the world than Doctor John Lyon and Fred Vinson. Fred and I played against each other when he was growing up at Louisa. Years later, I would visit him in Washington after he became chief justice of the Supreme Court, and he would remind me of those baseball days. 'Bryan,' he would say, 'we always had to play ten men when we played you at Paintsville— your team and that fellow you always ran in as umpire, Doctor Holbrook!'"

Doctor Hall's memory of athletics prompted C.V. Snapp to recall his experiences along those lines. "Van Lear had one of the first high school baseball teams in eastern Kentucky," the former school superintendent told us. "The town had a tradition of fielding fine teams, and they helped us in every way that they could. We established a football program in the high school as soon as possible. At first we didn't have enough boys to make a team, so we recruited some of the older fellows who went to school part time and mined coal part time." With this admission, Mister Snapp paused.

"We called them 'Bankmules,'" he said, chuckling, confirming

what my brother had told me many years earlier. "Bankmules!" he repeated proudly. "They sometimes called the coal mines 'banks' and the mine animals 'mules,'" he explained, and then, as if to correct any misunderstanding, he added, "Of course, these were not official games that first year, but then we became a Class A school the next year, and thereafter, as a member of the Big Sandy Conference, all of our games were official."

"Bankmule" remained a proud name until the school was merged into Johnson Central some forty

The three photos in this composite were made the year of the second big school reunion at Johnson Central. In the middle photo are Ann Beers (VLHS 1943), her Aunt Bertha Bradley McKay (VLHS 1924), and school superintendent C.V. Snapp. Below are Coach Vernon Honeycutt, Clyde Phelps (VLHS 1943), and Silva and Fannie Lyon.

years later. Jenkins' athletic teams opted for the nickname "Cavalier," the brand name used to identify the coking coal product from its mines. Had Van Lear teams been similarly designated, they would

At the upper left are Jim Kelly (VLHS 1954) and Janet Jasper Butcher (VLHS 1954); upper middle, Nicky Wetzel Pelphrey (VLHS 1954), Tom Wills (VLHS 1953), and Irene Wills; Kaye Stapleton (VLHS 1961) is pictured below Tom. All of these people played major roles in staging the school reunions. At the upper right, 1929 VLHS graduate and former county superintendent Virgil Porter addresses the 1992 school reunion group. Porter Elementary School has been named for him. In the next row at the left, Howard Sparks (VLHS 1934) receives the 2002 football award; to the right is Tom Wills, winner of the 2002 basketball award, surrounded by Van Lear basketball team members; at the right is Fred Wetzel (VLHS 1959), former high school principal and 2002 winner of the "Apple of your eye" award. In the next row, at the left, are two former school board members, Tom Meade (VLHS 1954), and Edgar Stapleton (VLHS 1931); in the middle are three former coaches, Eck Branham (1940-41), Vernon Honeycutt (1941-42), and Howard Ramey (1960s); and at the right are some of the awards donated and presented by Nicky Pelphrey to lucky winners who attended Van Lear school reunions from 1981-2002. At the lower left Tom Wills presents an award to me and Wanda Lee, for our contributions to the Van Lear town and school reunions from 1982-2000. At the lower right Sharon Fannin, Nicky Pelphrey, and Janet Jasper Butcher (VLHS 1954) present a check from the school reunion committee to the historical society.

have been known as "Grenadiers," the name used by Consol to market its Millers Creek coal.

When questioned about the attitude of the company toward education, Mister Snapp was quick to respond. "They supported us in every way," he said. "If a man didn't send his children to school, he was moved out."

In his interview, Virgil Porter, one of Snapp's students in the 1920s, who later became Johnson County school supervisor, had this to say about his schooling at Van Lear: "They had an excellent program then, and it would be a good one today. The high school taught physics and chemistry on alternate years, and biology and general science every year. Four English units were required, and the math program included two years of algebra, plane geometry, and trigonometry. You could get four units of science, four units of math, and four units of English. Latin was taught too. It was the only course in which I ever received a D. They taught vocal music, and Professor Snapp had two glee clubs in the school, in addition to a community chorus. We had dramatics, in fact just about everything you could want or needed in the way of college preparatory courses. The only shortfall was the lack of vocational courses. Typing, bookkeeping, and shorthand were taught, so I would say we were doing better than most public schools at that time. Remember, this was the 1920s."

Van Lear's Coach Eddie Congleton went on to become Dr. James E. Congleton, professor of English and Chairman of the Division of Humanities at Findlay College in Ohio. He came to Van Lear in 1925 following his graduation from Berea College. He received his MA from George Peabody in 1928, and became principal of Canton High School in Canton, Mississippi. Continuing his studies at the University of North Carolina, he was awarded his Ph.D. in 1936. After teaching in Turin, Italy, he spent twenty-two years as a professor at the University of Florida. There were other Van Lear teachers who were outstanding scholars, many of them recruited by Forest Pendleton Bell and C.V. Snapp.

Although Carlos V. Snapp served as superintendent of Van Lear Schools for only six years, his impact remained for many more. Born in Nicholas County, he was valedictorian of his Carlisle High School Class of 1912. After passing a teacher's exam, he taught for five years in his hometown school system before entering military service during World War I. When he completed his AB degree at the University of Kentucky in 1923, he came to Van Lear and remained there until 1929, when he went to Jenkins, spending the next 32 years in that system. He met and married Gussie Webb at Van Lear, where he also established a sterling reputation as an excellent school administrator. His wife worked alongside her husband in school, church, and community endeavors until her death in 1955. Snapp also served the Pike County Board of Education in various capacities until his retirement. When he returned to visit Van Lear in 1985 he had just celebrated his ninety-seventh birthday, and he could easily pass for a man still in his sixties.

Douglas Auxier Galbreath (VLHS 1926) and Virgil Porter (VLHS 1929).

Douglas Auxier and her brothers, Warren and Gene, were members of an old-line eastern Kentucky family. Their people were in eastern Kentucky back when the first settlement was established at Blockhouse Bottom. The Auxiers, along with the Prestons and a few other pioneer families did not succumb to the offers of the coal barons' land agents, electing instead to retain their fertile river farmland. Many of them did, however, avail themselves of the excellent new schools that had been established at Van Lear. Douglas recalled that her father, "took a job and moved us into one of the company houses so we might go to the Van Lear schools. Our schooling was quite good," she recalled. School records indicated that she and her brothers excelled. Douglas and Beulah Hammond, girlhood friends, were members of the school paper staff, and both took part in school plays and other activities. Years later Douglas owned and edited the county newspaper, and eventually retired to the family farm and restored the old farmhome.

Beulah Hammond Williamson spoke with great affection about her girlhood in Van Lear, where her father, John Hammond, worked in Mine No. 154 in 1914, and as a foreman at Mine No.152 in 1917. She recalled her good friend, Douglas Auxier, their work on the school paper, and her appearances in school plays. "In one play," she said, "I was Mini-Ha-Ha, and Lacy was Hiawatha." Lacy was Lacy Williamson, son of construction superintendent Joe Williamson. When Beulah and Lacy married in September 1926, they moved to Ashland.

Verne P. Horne served as head teacher at the Number Five School when C.V. Snapp was superintendent. "There were two things I will always remember about C.V. Snapp," he recalled. "One was his admonishment to us teachers that we must let the children know what an education ladder is, and we must teach them how to make progress toward a goal. Furthermore, we must let the children feel that they are helping us set the rules by which they must live. 'Of course,' he added, with a twinkle in his eye, 'we will make the rules, but we must make the youngsters feel that they are a part of the decision-making process.' "

"Those ideas," Horne said, "have stayed with me, and if I have made any contribution to education, these kinds of things have helped me do so."

Commenting on his experience while employed in the Van Lear schools, Horne stated, "Discipline was never a problem at Van Lear. We had the usual kinds of problems, some children occasionally playing hooky, but nothing like our problems out in the county." In searching for possible reasons for this, he echoed the remarks of others. "The company carefully selected the people who lived in their community," he said, "and the company wouldn't tolerate families who wouldn't send their children to school. Then too, we had an active PTA. Frank Cunningham was one of our first presidents. He, along with Mrs. E.W. Beers and others, gave us wonderful support."

Among the excellent teachers on Horne's faculty were Doris Hobson, Ethel Anderson, Bess Bradley, Alka Gibson, Elsie Webb, Clara Shaw, and Susie Risner. These quality teachers were later joined by Bessie Harris, Elizabeth Ladd, Ruth Brown, Elizabeth Wheatley, Ben Short, Sola Phillips, Ernest Thomas, Vaughn Lemaster, Virgil Preston, Harry Burchett, Mrs. Verne B. Horne, Mrs. L.B. Shepherd, Ruth Lanell Walters, Sally Wells, and a number of other local educators, all dedicated to the common goal of educating the young. Verne Horne served as superintendent of the Van Lear Schools following the tenure of Jesse Holland. Later, he became Johnson County school supervisor, succeeding Virgil Porter, who was honored years later when Porter Elementary School was named for him.

Members of old-line families expressed a variety of thoughts regarding the new coal town that came into their lives. The family of Milo Preston continued to operate their farm, near the mouth of Millers Creek. Son Jim, who now owns one of eastern Kentucky's leading funeral homes, recalled his early days. "Both my father and his father Clate sold produce from our farm," he told us. "I started setting milk on the porches of the houses at Van Lear when I was seven. We made two deliveries each day."

Jim Preston (VLHS 1946), seated center, the first president of the newly organized Van Lear Historical Society, at a Citizens National Bank book-signing. At the right is our good friend, Worth Goble (VLHS 1943).

When speaking on his family's long history in the region, Jim gave an intimate glimpse into his lineage and that of other families as well. "My grandfather Clate," Jim said, "married Priscilla Elliot, daughter of Abraham Elliot, who owned the farm and farmhouse across from the old Van Lear football field, where the Whitten coal tipple stands today. They sold that particular farm to the company. Later, at various times, the Snipes and Youngs lived there. The football boys used to go there to get a drink of fresh well water after a hard day's practice."

On his mother's side, Jim Preston's family goes back to the Blockhouse Bottom days at Harman Station. "My mother, Sally Auxier, was the daughter of Forest Lee (Dick) Auxier, and Vada Music Auxier," he continued. "Forest Lee's mother and father were Emily Spradlin and James K. Polk Auxier, who was a son of Agnes Wells and Samuel Auxier II." From his remarks it became clear that Jim was one of the few people that we would interview who had direct connections to the region's earliest white settlers.

James K. Polk Auxier's father, Samuel Auxier, was the fifth-born of Sarah (Sally) Brown and Samuel Auxier, Sr. This early Samuel Auxier was the youngest of six children of Michael Auxier of Auxerre, France, the original emigre Auxier. Michael fought with the French army in 1748 during the War of the Austrian Succession. Michael's son, the first Samuel, married Sarah Brown in 1779, and joined the Harmans at Blockhouse Bottom with the region's earliest settlers. Samuel II was twice married. His first marriage to Rebecca Phillips produced eleven children, the fourth a daughter, Sarah Auxier, who married George Washington Mayo, grandfather of J.C.C. Mayo. There were five children born to Samuel and his second wife, Agnes Wells, the fourth being James K. Polk Auxier, Jim Preston's maternal great grandfather.

Family ties dating this far back into America's early history become a bit confusing to all except those involved in genealogical research; however, it is not uncommon to find roots this deep among the people of Appalachia, as many descendants of early pioneer families found their way into the coal towns up and down the Big Sandy Valley. Thomas Wiley and his wife, the celebrated Jenny Sellards Wiley, overcame the trauma of Jenny's captivity by renegade Indians to raise another family of six children. Their daughter, Jennie, married Richard Williamson in 1810, and their descendants scattered throughout the upper reaches of Tug River country. A younger daughter married a Borders, and many of their offspring remained in Johnson County. On the Sellards side, at least one of the descendants of old Hezekiah Sellards, who was Jenny Wiley's father, became a Van Lear coal miner. John Sellards remained there for a good part of his life, raising his family and sending them to Van Lear schools, and it was his daughter Maxine who had been my grade school classmate.

By 1920, Van Lear boasted a population of 3,000, greater than any other town in Johnson County, including Paintsville, the county seat. Automobiles had begun to appear on the rocky roads, as improvements continued along Millers Creek. Landscaping was added around the new recreation building, stores and clubhouse; garden space was provided near miners' homes, and a program of recreation and entertainment was initiated. Living in one of Consolidation Coal Company's Kentucky towns was not bad in the first quarter of the twentieth century. You could do worse—much worse—at that particular time in the history of this country.

A number of the early issues of *The Bankmule*, the new historical society's quarterly newsletter, were devoted to the "olden days." The December 1987 and March 1988 issues told about early landmarks no longer extant and people who played important roles in the town. In the December 1987 *Bankmule*,

Paul Greene and Jim Kelly.

James Paul Greene told of his family's moving to Van Lear in 1913 when the general manager's house and the club house stood atop Club House Hill overlooking the Big Sandy River, as the Levisa Fork was commonly known. The Millers Creek Railroad's passenger train made regular stops at the water tower and power station across from these two houses, which could be reached by way of a wooden stairway or a winding dirt road. According to Greene, there were two tennis courts on the hill, and it was likely that Hampton Kemper,

At the upper left is Bertha Bradley, with Silva Lyon's sister Beatrice at her left. Bess Bradley is the young girl holding the infant.

Lacy Williamson, Clifford Meddings, and Clyde Sparks played there, along with others, mostly young "white-collar Company employees who had been transferred or imported from other places."

Bertha Bradley McKay, born in 1904, moved with her family to Van Lear in 1909. She recalled, "To get to the Club House, we took a road between the first and second row of houses at the River, that led to the top of the hill (if going by horseback). To walk to the building, there was a board walk and then eight steps and a platform; in all there may have been 100 steps, and several platforms on the way up. There was another walk path on the other side of the hill." She stated that the first manager of the Club House was the mother of Wyona Berlin, and the second manager, Mary Dixon.

While still in his teens, James Paul Greene was hired to help with the building of the "new" clubhouse next to the recreation building. He believed it was 1923, having arrived at the date based on his recollection that this was the year he suffered a cut when he fell from his perch on the second floor to the concrete basement.

Mina Duty Cubbon, a resident of Tallahassee, Florida, wrote about her memories of Van Lear and the Club House. "The most loving, hard-working, and loyal people I have ever known," she said, "were my Daddy, A.C. Duty, my mother, Cora Duty, and my 'Aunt Dosh,' Mae Duty.

"My family moved to Van Lear in 1932 when Daddy went there to be manager of Consolidation Coal Company's Recreation Hall. My mother worked with Daddy in the Recreation Hall, and Aunt Dosh kept house for the three of them. They lived in a house just within walking distance of both the Club House and the Recreation Building.

The clubhouse at Van Lear around 1960, shortly after the structure had been remodeled by its new owner. It later burned, but during our youth, this building was the scene of many lively "proms" and parties.

"Aunt Dosh had lived with us since I was born. She had made a home for her father, my grandfather, in Oakland, Maryland, in earlier years. Andrew Woodbury Duty was a Civil War veteran, and was in Andersonville Prison Camp in Georgia when the war ended. When I was born in 1910, three days before Grandfather died, my Daddy, Aunt Dosh, and their brother were at his bedside. Grandfather said, 'I want to know that Dosh will have a home with one of you boys when I am gone.' Aunt Dosh chose the Alf Duty home because there was a new baby. B.L. Duty's household did not have any children.

"Certainly one of Aunt Dosh's main traits was that of service. This is the background for what happened in late 1935. Consolidation Coal Company always had faith in the Duty family; both A.C. and his brother, Ben (B.L.) had served them well for many years in West Virginia. It was natural that when Mrs. Stump, who had been managing the Club House until late 1935, decided to leave and go to Pennsylvania, the Company should turn to the Dutys for help. They asked Cora to take over managing the Club House, but continue to work with Daddy in the Recreation Hall as well. She would still make her famous vegetable soup and hot-dog sauce for the lunch counter. Aunt Dosh was offered the position of head cook at the Club House, and the three of them—Daddy, Mother, and Aunt Dosh—would move into the Club House to live.

"At the time the offer was made, Aunt Dosh was in Morgantown, West Virginia, with my husband and me; we were expecting a baby any day. Nancy Cubbon was born on December 19, 1935."

Alfa Duty Barnes, also then living in Tallahassee, recalled when Consol officials came to Van Lear from Fairmont, West Virginia in 1935 to ask her mother, Mrs. Alf Duty, to manage the new Club House, a position she held until the early 1940s. She described the building and its use. "A large front door opened into the lobby, and in the middle of the room was a banquet-sized table. There were leather-covered settees and chairs, and rugs lay scattered on the highly polished wooden floor.

"To the left of the lobby was a suite of bedrooms, and a bath. Company officials stayed there when they came to Van Lear. The dining room to the right of the lobby contained four large tables, each capable of seating ten or twelve people. An oversized cupboard which held clean linen and silverware stood against one wall. A swinging door led to the roomy kitchen where there was a big coal stove, double sinks, a long work table, and a small table and chairs. Half of one wall was lined with top and bottom cabinets, and a pantry with a restaurant-sized refrigerator. The back door led to a small enclosure, and steps gave access to sunken garbage cans. A stairway inside the kitchen led down to the basement, where the washing was done, and the coal furnace was housed. The manager's private residence was off the kitchen to the left. Our parents lived in this apartment, which consisted of a bedroom, bath, and sitting room. These rooms also opened into the lobby.

"Stairs from the lobby led to the second floor, which housed the men who lived at the Club House. There was one large bathroom containing three or four shower stalls and other appointments. There were seven or eight single rooms, and at the end of the hall was another suite of rooms with a single bath between.

"The third floor was for the women. There was one double bedroom, and four singles, and one large, multiple bathroom. Each room was furnished with bed, dresser, desk, and chair. Simple, but quite comfortable."

Numerous individuals had good things to say about Jack Price. All of them affirmed that, during her best years, from 1914 to 1934, Van Lear was widely regarded as a wonderful place to live and work, largely because of the management and groundwork laid by Superintendent Price, who set the standards for others to follow. His most noteworthy achievement was the establishment of rigorous screening of the men and families who were employed in the town. There were hundreds of early pioneer families who had one or more members employed as coal miners, and many of those family names may still be found throughout eastern Kentucky. They include the Adams, Andersons, Auxiers, Bevins, Blairs, Blevins, Borders, Bowlings, Browns, Burchetts, Burkes, Burketts, Burtons, Butchers,

Butlers, Cantrells, Castles, Caudills, Cecils, Chandlers, Clays, Collins, Colvins, Daniels, Davises, Dickersons, Dixons, Fairchilds, Franklins, Gobles, Hagers, Hammonds, Harrises, Hayburns, Hitchcocks, Hobsons, Holbrooks, Honeycutts, Hornes, Huffs, Hydens, Kazees, Kellys, Kings, LeMasters, Lynns, Lyons, Marshalls, Mays, Mayos, McCoarts, Meades, Meddings, Meeks, Mollettes, Murrays, Musics, O'Bryans, Pelphreys, Phelps, Picklesimers, Porters, Prestons, Prices, Rameys, Ratliffs, Rices, Ruperts, Salyers, Sellards, Setsers, Shorts, Skaggs, Smiths, Sparks, Spears, Spradlins, Staffords, Stambaughs, Stapletons, Sturgills, Tacketts, Thackers, Trimbles, Turners, VanHooses, Vaughans, Walkers, Wards, Webbs, Wells, Wheelers, Wileys, Williams, Williamsons, and Youngs.

Workers in the Van Lear mines were a mixture of native Anglo-Saxons, like those named, and miners and their families who were either foreign-born, or first or second-generation U.S. citizens. In 1984, Jeanette Knowles transcribed more than sixty names from Catholic Church burial records, and published them in *The Bankmule*. Among those in this latter group, now deceased and buried in the Van Lear Catholic Cemetery, were Lorenz Guidera, Joseph Pickutovski, Stanislaus Doperyski, Laurrutuis Czaikowski, Paulus Kasiak, John Gaiski, Walter Lomnicki, Michael Lavko, George Sotnikoff, and Alexandra Platkus. Other residents of European lineage included the Campigottos, Perkoskis, Leminskis, Marinos, Gibroskis, and Verbonics. The list spanned more than fifty years, from 1911 through 1966.

What was a miner's life like? Interviews with former miner-residents give insights. For one thing, there was never a lot of money around. Although miners were usually well-paid in relation to other tradesmen, their pay was dependent upon the price of coal on the open market and the relationship of miner to employer. When Henry Ford announced his "Five Dollar Day" for his workers, the Van Lear coal loader usually earned more than that in a given day. At times, when the price of coal was high, they earned considerably more, but rarely enough to compensate for the additional danger and discomfort they endured.

Paul Wetzel, Nicky's father, who entered the employ of Consol in the Van Lear mines at age 17.

In the December 1986 issue of *The Bankmule*, Jeanette Knowles reported on her interviews with George Davis and Aud Williamson, both of whom had worked in the Van Lear mines. Davis' family owned property along the Big Sandy River, near West Van Lear. The first road into Van Lear from Paintsville traversed their property and was known as the Davis Branch Road. Davis said that he began working in Mine No. 151 in 1910 when he was 21 years of age. He described how men drilled a hole about five feet into the solid coal, and then inserted a cartridge of black powder rolled into a newspaper, and a two-foot-long squid or fuse. The ensuing explosion usually broke the coal into loadable pieces.

The industry-wide strike of 1919 led to higher coal prices and wages, but foreign oil became a cheaper alternative fuel, forcing both prices and wages back down. Despite occasional "boomlets" during the 1920s, the country's economy faltered, the stock market

Artifacts of the Van Lear Local Union #5835 of the United Mine Workers of America.

crashed in 1929, and the Great Depression followed. Despite the best efforts of both management and labor, Consolidation Coal Company faltered financially and went into receivership on June 3, 1932. The Depression continued without letup through the decade of the 1930s, ending only with the onset of World War II. In 1933, the first year of Franklin D. Roosevelt's first term as president, the price of coal plummeted when marginal operators could find no buyers. Larger, more substantial companies like Consol retaliated, cutting their prices to move coal to market. The coal loader's wage per ton was cut accordingly. It was then evident that the nationwide economic depression had reached the coal fields. Everyone hoped that somehow, perhaps through the U.M.W. and the new Roosevelt administration, the nation's fortunes could be turned around. The new president's popularity among most miners was widespread, if not universal. Indeed, his popularity among them was probably second only to that of John L. Lewis, this in spite of the fact that the miners' fortunes had worsened, rather than improved since FDR was elected. Somehow, most miners sensed that the man in the White House was on their side. Programs were being proposed to aid the working man and the nation's economy.

In addition to the Wagner Act, which guaranteed collective bargaining, and a new unemployment insurance program, workers soon gained other benefits under Roosevelt. Public works programs put thousands of previously unemployed men to work. They built schools, roads, and parks. The stone gymnasium at Van Lear was one such project constructed by the W.P.A. Gradually, things began to improve for miners who worked for Consol. Following a period of reorganization, the company's capitalization was restructured, and mining operations were resumed at most locations, but on a considerably reduced work schedule of from two to three days per week for most miners.

George Davis said that, when he commenced working at Van Lear, small ponies were used to haul the coal to the higher-roofed area of the main haulage, where an electric motor pulled the cars outside the mine to the tipple. Davis said that the coal in Mine No. 151 was lower than in any other Van Lear mine, averaging around thirty inches, whereas the coal in Mine No. 154 was twice that height in places. He said that the low coal and the difficulty encountered in mining it was probably the reason Mine No. 151 was closed in 1931. This bit of information agrees with my memory of my father's taking me back into this mine during that particular summer, when Dad and his fellow workers were employed to collapse the main entryway with explosives, thus bringing to an end any further mining by Consol. Years later, after the Company sold off its properties, Pat McCoart re-opened Mine No. 151 for a short time.

Reflecting on his mining career, Davis said a workday could run to ten or twelve hours until unionization came in 1933. His pay at Jenkins had averaged about $1.75 a day. When he and his cousin Frank, along with John Mollette and other miners decided that they wanted to meet to discuss joining the union, they had to cross Johns Creek Hill, away from Company property. When the union did come to Van Lear, Superintendent J.D. Snyder cut 300 workers because they did not live in town. George Davis, who was then living on Fitch Branch, was one of the men cut from the payroll at that time. He celebrated his 98th birthday on December 25, 1996. Born December 25, 1898, at Meally, he died May 26, 1997, seven months short of reaching his 99th.

Tubby Harris recalled that Finley Jarrell took him into Mine No. 151 when he was about eight years old, and his experience was similar to mine. After it was closed, he and his friends sometimes rode the abandoned mine cars down the slope to the tipple. In the same issue of *The Bankmule*, Tom Goble's daughter, Marie Hall, recalled that her husband, Cecil Hall, helped pull pillars in 1950 when Pat McCoart assumed the Far West lease, and hired men to go with him by way of the old airway to do additional mining. Jeff Stratton described how Kenneth Russell Webb played around the Number 1 mine, and he told about the mining experiences of his uncle, Estill Stacy, and Estill's father-in-law, William Stratton.

Aud Williamson recalled that he first worked in Mine No. 155, and in time in all the other mines at Van Lear. He said that his job at Mine No. 151 was to load coal and to run the tram motor when the brakeman was absent. He also recalled that Mine No. 151 was closed during the summer of 1931. He said that it remained idle until 1950 when Far West Coal Company leased all of the mines from Consol, and workers for that company pulled pillars from mines 1, 4, and 5. Aud Williamson said that he joined Pat McCoart, Opal Dawson, and others in 1950, pulling pillars in Mine No. 151 for about one mile inside the entry. Since the track had not been pulled, it was removed and sold as scrap before the second closing of this mine. Williamson then worked in Breathitt County until his retirement. .

Ed Hayburn, who lived and worked in Van Lear throughout most of his adult life, maintained a record book of union membership and company service to assist miners with their black-lung

Aud Williamson's home at the left. The house at the right was the one occupied by the Doctor John Lyon family in 1916.

Ed Hayburn and Bruce Phelps, charter members of Van Lear Local Union #5835 of the UMW. This photo appeared in the March 1984 issue of The Bankmule.

claims, following his retirement. He gave good marks to both Consol and Van Lear miners. Consol ran a good town, he recalled. "If the coal hadn't been so low, I would say Van Lear would have been the best of the better coal towns."

The Van Lear that evolved following its abandonment by Consolidation Coal Company continued as an incorporated entity and, as we have seen, prospered for a time, even winning an award in the 1960s as a model town for municipalities having a population under 2,500. The town voted in 1965 to dissolve its charter and become unincorporated, only to vote to reincorporate in 1991. Paul Deaton, a former Johnson County Commonwealth Attorney, was appointed mayor, and immediately took steps to enforce litter laws, and collect modest assessments in property taxes.

At the top of this three-part composite photo are Jim Kelly, Joyce McAllister Meade, and Joyce's husband, Tommy Meade (all VLHS 1954), longtime volunteer workers in the Van Lear Historical Society; in the middle photo are three of Greene Conley's children, Charles (VLHS 1942), Stewart (VLHS 1936), and Sophia Conley; and, in the lower section, a portion of a school reunion group.

At the top Warren "Tubby" Harris (VLHS 1935) and his wife, Carrie Cecil Harris (VLHS 1936), are greeted by a party in the old office building. Early residents, the couple returned to Van Lear and bought and refurbished one of the nicer homes, following Warren's retirement as a federal mine inspector. Tubby became active in the activities of the historical society, and in year-2000 he was recognized as a "Hometown Hero" by television station WSAZ in Huntington, West Virginia. The middle photo shows him receiving the award, with friends looking on.

These photos show former Van Lear High School cheerleaders, being recognized at one of the school reunions (top), with other reunion guests pictured below.

The latter offended Paul David Butcher, owner of the local cable television facility, who told *Lexington Herald-Leader* reporter Lee Mueller, "The people of Van Lear do not want to live in an incorporated city." A petition was circulated calling for a referendum on the issue, and the town once again decided to unincorporate by a vote of 275 to 203. Van Lear's population had dwindled down to slightly more than 1600 people in 1994 at the time of the referendum.

The Van Lear Historical Society owes its success to those few individuals who have worked diligently—at this writing for twenty years—to save the old office building, establish a museum, and keep members informed with their publication of *The Bankmule*, the quarterly first begun by Jeanette Knowles and Danny Blevins and continued through the years by Joyce McCallister Meade, Warren "Tubby" Harris, Mary Richmond, Glenna Music, Iris Ward Blair, Janet Jasper Butcher, and a handful of other volunteers, including all the people who gave of their time to lead the society as its president—Jim Preston; Bill and Garnetta Rucker; Doug, Louise, and B.B. Kretzer; Jim Kelly; Tim Barker; and Danny Blevins.

At the upper left are some of the people who were instrumental in the founding of the non-profit Van Lear Historical Society. Honored at the 2000 school reunion, left to right, are James Vaughan, Jim Kelly, Wanda Lee Vaughan, Joyce McCallister Meade, Edgar Stapleton, Garnetta Wells Rucker, Iris Ward Blair, Louise King Kretzer, and Charles Spears. At the upper right is Charles Spears (VLHS 1945), former C&O Yardmaster at Paintsville, who obtained an old C&O railroad caboose for the society. The photo in the middle left was taken in the 1980s shortly after the old Consol office building received a new coat of paint. At the right are Bill and Garnetta Wells Rucker (VLHS 1944), and Wanda Lee and Jim Vaughan, taking a break from their work on the Van Lear town model. At the lower left, George Vaughan (VLHS 1932) and John Ward stand in the old Masonic room across from the town model, a portion of which is pictured at the right.

In 1989 I visited the Big Pit Mine at

Bill Rucker, early president of the Van Lear Historical Society and longtime volunteer worker, stands in front of a portion of the "Veterans Wall of Fame." Two memorials added during the administration of Danny Blevins are shown below. It has been said that Johnson County probably sent more sons off to World War II than any other county in the nation.

Blaenavon in southern Wales. Although it closed as a working colliery in 1980, a hundred years after its first commercial use as a source of both coal and ironstone, former underground miners refused to let their beloved mine die. Instead, they banded together to form the Big Pit Museum Trust, an "independent charitable body" whose avowed purpose is to "preserve the historic pit as part of the heritage of South Wales." For a modest admission fee, visitors don

Flanked by two Welsh miners, Bobby Ascione and I prepare to descend to the depths of the Big Pit mine at Blaenavon in southern Wales. The year is 1989, a week after Wanda Lee and I took the town model to Van Lear.

a safety helmet, cap lamp, and "self-rescuer," and under the supervision of former miners, tour the Big Pit Mine to a depth of three hundred feet, to see coal faces and haulage equipment. Ventilation doors, stables for ponies which were once used as draft animals, and the working sites in both the coal and iron ore sections are maintained as in days of yore. Above ground is a canteen and gift shop.

Closer to Van Lear is Blue Heron, a mining town long defunct,

The railroad trestle and a portion of the reconstructed mine tipple at Blue Heron in McCreary County Kentucky.

and much smaller than Van Lear even in its productive days, but the beneficiary of the goodwill, guiding hands, and generosity of both a friendly federal and state government, and the heirs of the family who once controlled the town and its mines. Although nothing remains of the original buildings or mines, symbolic recreations dramatically present the town as it once was. This writer was first made aware of Blue Heron when reading the August 1989 issue of *Southern Living* magazine, which included an article describing both the unique English-like community of Rugby in Tennessee and the Big South Fork National River and Recreation Area in McCreary County, Kentucky, a huge area encompassing thousands of acres in both states. Rescued from inundation by a dam which would have been constructed on the Cumberland River, Blue Heron was included in a massive federal and state-funded project to save the area from further exploitation. Although all of the original mining structures were gone, many representational recreations were designed and built upon their original sites, where audio tapes made by some of the town's residents tell of their memories of the town and its past glory. A good place to start a tour is at the Stearns Museum, housed in a building donated by the mine-owner family, after which you can board the Big South Fork Scenic Railway for a scenic ride to Blue Heron, where you will find a massive coal tipple and tram bridge, and an interpretive center and depot, in addition to the representative structures.

Thanks mostly to the efforts of one former resident, the relatively small mining town of Boissevain in Tazewell County, Virginia, survived as a tourist attraction after its mining days ended in 1956. David Phipps, a native of Boissevain, returned there in 1984 after concluding a successful career with a large corporation. The eighth of thirteen children and the son of a retired Boissevain miner, he found himself standing on a hill overlooking the old mine when it occurred to him that something should be done to honor the memory of thirty-eight miners who lost their lives in a gas explosion in that mine on the morning of February 28, 1932, three years before the gas explosion that took the lives of nine Van Lear miners. In 1985, Phipps and four other locals, mostly retired miners, began to discuss ideas, finally settling on a plan to establish a fund at a local bank. The fund began to grow rather quickly, although not always easily. They first purchased a six-acre sludge pond which had been used as a garbage heap. Their area Congressman, Rick Boucher, was made honorary chairman of their new non-profit Boissevain Coal Miners' Memorial Museum and Park, Inc. The Virginia National Guard was invited to come and help. Not once, but twice this group came in, cut trees, and bulldozed and moved hilltops to fill in the sludge pond. Three years later, Consolidation Coal Company brought in equipment, finished filling the pond, and reseeded the new surface. Consol continued to donate old mining equipment for outdoor display, and added an additional seven acres of land as the site for the new miner's museum. "Without the coal operators," Phipps is quoted as saying, "there would be no coal miner and vice-

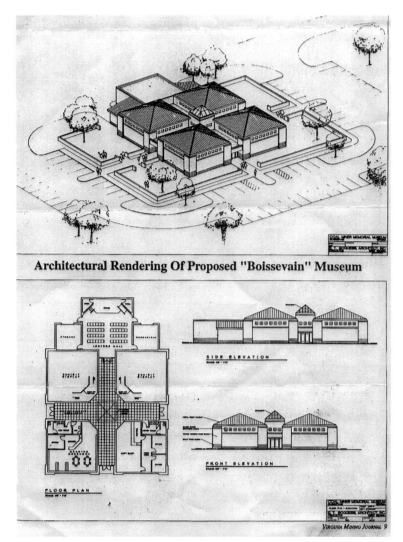

Architectural Rendering Of Proposed "Boissevain" Museum

An architect's sketch of the proposed Boissevain Museum project.

versa." To date much remains to be completed, but work continues. It is significant and noteworthy that the same employer has not been solicited for similar assistance at Van Lear.

None of these old mining towns that are being successfully restored to productive lives rivals Van Lear in terms of size or importance as coal-mining enterprises. Not one can be said to be more worthy of restoration. Yet the Big Pit in southern Wales, Boissevain in Tazewell County, Virginia, and Blue Heron in southern Kentucky have far exceeded Van Lear in terms of the amount of public, private, and governmental support that each has received. I am unable to determine why this is so, although the failure to reincorporate the town and thus provide a measure of stability is bound to have played a role. To date, the Van Lear Historical Society has received a great deal of in-kind help from a few individuals who have labored selflessly to raise funds through various events and who provide much-needed services to publish the newsletter and maintain the old office building for meetings and tours of the museum. Modest amounts of money have been received from private donors, including bequests from the estate of former school superintendent Verne P. Horne, and from the family of the late Jim Pelphrey. The largest government grant, $25,000, came from the Commonwealth of Kentucky, thanks to the good work of State Senator Benny Ray Bailey and State Representative Johnny Ray Turner. Governor Paul Patton made the presentation to VLHS President Danny K. Blevins at the Senior Citizens' Center in Paintsville, April 16, 2001. This sum was put to good use for much-needed repair work on the museum building and community park. A PRIDE grant was also being sought with which to construct a sewage system.

Several other mining towns in eastern Kentucky have put together boot-strap organizations in efforts to save their communities. Homeowners in Auxier, in Floyd County, have done a good job of restoring their homes, and leveling most of those that were derelict. Jenkins, another Kentucky mining town built by Consol in Letcher County, created its own video, narrated by former superintendent David Zegeer. Benham and Lynch in Harlan County have witnessed self-help efforts over the years but, as is the case with Van Lear, it is difficult to sustain such undertakings.

The efforts of the valiant volunteers who have struggled to preserve Van Lear via the museum and historical society have not gone unrecognized by news media in the area. Shortly after the formation of the society, the July 21, 1982 edition of the *Paintsville Herald* carried an impressive full-page spread of old photographs and an article by Jeanette Knowles in which she described the plans for the society and a second school reunion. Seventeen years later, the April 23, 1999, *Floyd County Times* ran a cover story in its TV insert, featuring photos of the scale model and items from the museum. At least two web sites on the internet are devoted to the town and VLHS.

As this is written, no corporate or government funding of any magnitude has been made available to the few volunteers who continue to struggle to keep the history of the town of Van Lear alive. At least one thing now seems certain regarding any possible funding assistance from the federal government. With the destruction of the twin World Trade Center buildings in New York City, the war in Afghanistan, and the uncertainties in the Middle East, federal attention and funds will quite naturally be focused on these overriding national needs, rather than on projects to save old towns like Van Lear. I would only suggest that the need to retain, preserve, and restore good things from our past also deserves a high priority, perhaps now more than ever.

If much of what I have written in this book is simple nostalgia, so be it, but I also feel that I have told of a time when Americans, although perhaps exploited, were happier in their work and leisure hours, when American society was nobler, less rapacious and greedy, and perhaps more mannerly or even courtly. Some will say that this is nonsense. One older lady who had grown up under circumstances similar to mine rejected any such allusions to the 1930s as "the good old days," reminding me that women back then worked from dawn to dusk, scrubbing clothes on wash boards, cooking three meals a day over hot coal-fired cook stoves, and "making do" with whatever their men provided for them and their families. Touché! The age of the plastic credit card is better in that regard. But, I still maintain that something really bad happened to us when mama went to work full-time. Some will understand what I mean when I say that I long for a return to Victorian Hypocrisy, an age when we may not have been the sort of people we appeared to be, but at least we were all expected to conduct ourselves with a certain propriety and sense

Mine tipple #154 is in the foreground, and tipple #153, Slate Row, and Music Holler beyond. Wolfpen Holler is just out of view to the right of the #154 tipple. Near this site a quantity of Millers Creek block coal was removed in 1908 and hauled by team and wagon to Stafford, Kentucky. The blocks were then shipped on two rail cars to Jamestown, Virginia, where they were used to construct a coal house, which proved to be one of the major attractions at the Jamestown Exposition of 1908. Our sandlot teams knew nothing about this bit of history when we played baseball near here in the 1930s.

of decency. For those who do not understand this, no amount of explaining will change their opinion.

As I bring down the final curtain on the story of my life and my personal involvement in the later life of my hometown, it occurs to me that what this little book has been "about" more than any other single thing is a longing for what many of us who grew up in company towns like Van Lear regard as a better way of life. What we miss most of all are all the good ways and habits that many Americans enjoyed in years gone by, social values and demeanor that we have abandoned over the years, some of a serious nature, others perhaps now considered trivial, yet those ways of living were significant in that they contributed to what I have characterized as a "happier" time. To help illustrate what I mean, how long has it been since you sat in a swing on a porch or on a stoop or a rail or a curb or on the grass, and just sat there, perhaps alone with your thoughts, or with a friend, looking up at the sky and guessing the shapes of clouds? And do you remember penny candy, Hide-and-Go-Seek, playing baseball without adult supervision, family dinners, hop-scotch, climbing trees, homemade shows, cowboys and Indians, funny valentines, the Depression, World War II, men who tipped their hats to ladies, taking pride in your job, proud railroad engineers who wore striped caps, and people who whistled while they worked? How about walking to the movie theater or walking just about anywhere without fear, laughing a lot, leaving your keys in the car and your front door unlocked, usually finding your mom when you needed her, hoping you wouldn't find either parent after you had violated a rule at school, earning a dime or a quarter for doing work around the house, innocent violence-free movies, "watching" the radio? All of these things were part of the life that we knew every day in the Van Lear that I remember. I have tried to set down here my recollections of that life as a record and a reminder of all that we who lived in Van Lear—and other towns like it—enjoyed at one time.

Photographic

Appendix

VLHS = Van Lear Historical Society

Silva and Fannie Lyon, longtime VLHS supporters.

Jim Kelly, former VLHS president.

Mary Pack Richmond, VLHS worker.

B.B. Kretzer, former VLHS president.

Louise King Kretzer, former VLHS president.

Doug Kretzer (VLHS 1967), former VLHS president.

Danny Blevins, worker.

Phyllis Blevins, worker.

Sue Conley, worker and singer.

Neva Jean Selvidge Barker (VLHS 1943), worker.

Tim Barker, past president of VLHS.

Danny Blevins, two-time president of VLHS, accepting a check from Kentucky Governor Patton.

Brothers Marcus and Charles Spears, VLHS workers.

The first Van Lear club house atop the hill at the river is pictured here on a snowy day a few years before it burned. It was here that my father and I cut our Christmas tree in December of 1934, a year before Dad's death in the Van Lear mines.

Young Russell May sits in his homemade cart and guides his bankmule, a hard-working animal whose services were no longer needed in the mines around 1918.

(above) *Members of the Bluegrass group "Five Miles from Nowhere" pose in front of the old priest home at Van Lear for the cover photo on their album "Lonesome Old Home." Members of the group are David Hall (mandolin), Hack Thornberry (fiddle), Jack Howard (bass), Jimmy Lee (banjo), and Donald Witten (guitar VLHS 1968). The equal of many Nashville groups, bookings may be arranged through Jim Lee at 805 Ridgeway Drive, Paintsville, Kentucky 41240, telephone 606-789-6662.*

(above opposite) *Coach Eck Branham and Van Lear High School's last official Bankmule football team in September of 1940. Members of that team are identified within the context of this book, although not all of the players are seen in this photo.*

(below opposite) *Van Lear miners Jake Wills and Emerson Jennings take a break from coal-cutting operations. The coal seam is about 30-inches thick. Approximately the same thickness of slate has been taken in order to create five feet of headroom. Most of the Miller's Creek coal was thin and difficult to mine. c. 1922*

This composite photo shows a number of Van Lear's athletic teams. Down the left side, beginning at the upper left, is the last official Bankmule football team coached in 1940 by Eck Branham (center); below them is a young team coached by Jesse Holland around 1932, with Tubby Harris holding the football; below that photo is another early 1920s team; and three 1940 - 41 cheerleaders, Eloise Hall, Naomi Rucker, and Jenny Meddings. Down the center, starting at the top, is our 1940 basketball team, which went down in defeat in the district tournament to the Inez Indians, who then captured the overall Kentucky State High School Basketball Championship; immediately below that team are some members of our 1941 team; below them are four members of the same team; at the bottom are baseball players Virgil Burkett and Pat McCoart. Down the right side, at the top are some members of the 1928 football team; below them are three of Van Lear's better baseball teams.

About the
Author

James Vaughan was born and reared in eastern Kentucky. He attended Michigan State College and served in the U.S. Navy during World War II, achieving the rank of lieutenant (jg). He graduated from Oklahoma University in 1947 with a B.A. in mathematics and physics. In 1962 he received the MSE degree. He managed a commercial broadcast station in Miami, Florida, for a time, moving with his wife, Wanda Lee (Rice) Vaughan, to an Arkansas rice farm in 1955, where he has lived for almost 50 years, teaching and writing. He served as a member of the Arkansas Educational Television Commission from 1980 - 1988, and played a major role in establishing a statewide academic competition known as *Quiz Bowl*. He has authored 60 instructional books. His first work of fiction, a political story titled *The Polemicists*, won the 1993 Heartland Writers' Guild award for Contemporary Fiction. In 1996 his mystery story, "The Case of La Grande Dame," was selected for publication from more than 300 submissions to *The New Yorker* magazine. *Bankmules* is his most recent work. He is currently working on a novel.

Nonfiction publication credits include:

"A Study of Vocabulary Improvement Techniques," *NSPI Journal* (National Society for Programmed Instruction) 8 (no.6), 1968
Mr. Ready, AudioActive, Inc., 1975
Mr. Phun Phonics, AudioActive, Inc., 1979

Ceres: A Space Odyssey, AudioActive, Inc., 1984 (This software program for Apple II computers was included in NASA's *Second Edition of Software for Aerospace Education*, 1990, p. 24, Section I)

Blue Moon Over Kentucky: *A biography of Kentucky's Troubled Highlands*, Delapress, Inc., 1985